Shirley Fretz
Box 23
Mattru, Jong

West African Nature Handbooks
General Editor: *H. J. Savory, M.Sc.*

WEST AFRICAN SNAKES

G. S. CANSDALE
B.A., B.SC., F.L.S.

ILLUSTRATED BY JOHN NORRIS WOOD

LONGMANS

LONGMANS, GREEN AND CO. LTD
48 Grosvenor Street, London W.1

*Associated companies, branches and representatives
throughout the world*

© G. S. Cansdale 1961

First published 1961

Reprinted 1965

Other titles in the series
WEST AFRICAN LILIES AND ORCHIDS
SMALL MAMMALS OF WEST AFRICA
BIRDS OF THE WEST AFRICAN TOWN AND GARDEN

*Made and printed in Great Britain by
William Clowes and Sons, Limited, London and Beccles*

CONTENTS

I.	SNAKES IN NATURE	1
II.	SNAKES IN WEST AFRICA: FREQUENCY, SOCIAL AND ECONOMIC IMPORTANCE	9
III.	THE PYTHON FAMILY	16
	The African or Rock Python	16
	The Royal Python	19
	The Calabar Ground Python	21
	The Sand Boa	22
IV.	HARMLESS SNAKES	23
	The Worm Snakes	24
	The Spotted Blind Snake	26
	The Red-lined Snake	27
	Smyth's Water Snake	27
	The Brown Water Snake	29
	The West African House Snake	29
	The File Snake	30
	The Black Tree Snake	31
	The Egg-eating Snake	32
	The African Green Snakes	33
	The Green-lined Snake	35
	The Emerald Snake	35
	The White-spotted Beaked Snake	35
	The Cocoa Farm Snake	35
	The White-spotted Snake	36
V.	BACK-FANGED SNAKES	36
	The African Beauty Snake (Plain form)	38
	The African Beauty Snake (Striped form)	38
	The Rufous Beaked Snake	39

CONTENTS

The Cat Snake	40
The Boomslang	40
The Burrowing Snake	41
The Twig Snake	42
Blanding's Tree Snake	43
The Powdery Tree Snake	44

VI. COBRAS AND MAMBAS — 44

The Green Mambas	45
The Black-necked or Spitting Cobra	48
The Black Cobra	50
The Egyptian Cobra	53
The Hoodless Cobra	54
The Water Cobra	55
The Black Garter Snake	56

VII. VIPERS — 56

The Night Adder	57
The Puff Adder	59
The Gaboon Viper	60
The Rhinoceros Viper	62
The Green Tree Viper	63
The Carpet Viper	64
The Horned or Sand Viper	65
The Burrowing Vipers	66

VIII. SNAKE BITE—ITS PREVENTION AND TREATMENT — 69

LIST OF ILLUSTRATIONS

		between pages
PLATE I	Royal Python	18 & 19
	African or Rock Python	
PLATE II	Sand Boa	18 & 19
	Calabar Ground Python	
PLATE III	Red-lined Snake	18 & 19
	Spotted Blind Snake	
PLATE IV	Smyth's Water Snake	18 & 19
	Brown Water Snake	
PLATE V	Green-lined Snake	34 & 35
	Emerald Snake	
	West African House Snake	
	File Snake	
PLATE VI	Egg-eating Snake	34 & 35
	Black Tree Snake—Juvenile	
	Black Tree Snake—Adult	
PLATE VII	Twig or Vine Snake	34 & 35
	African Beauty Snake—Plain Form	
	African Beauty Snake—Striped Form	
PLATE VIII	Rufous Beaked Snake	34 & 35
	The Burrowing Snake	
PLATE IX	Blanding's Tree Snake—Black and Brown Varieties	42 & 43
	Boomslang	
PLATE X	Green Mamba	42 & 43
	Hoodless Cobra	
PLATE XI	Spitting Cobra	58 & 59
	Black Cobra	
PLATE XII	Puff Adder	58 & 59
	Egyptian Cobra	

v

LIST OF ILLUSTRATIONS

		between pages
PLATE XIII	Green Tree Viper	66 & 67
	Burrowing Viper	
	Night Adder	
PLATE XIV	Gaboon Viper	66 & 67
	Rhinoceros Viper	
PLATE XV	Carpet Viper	66 & 67
	Horned or Sand Viper	

NOTES

1. The number shown on the plates beside the illustrations refers to the number of the description in the text.

2. The use of initial capital letters for English snake names mentioned in the text denotes an accepted popular name.

*To my wife,
who even lets me keep snakes
in the drawing-room.*

CHAPTER I

SNAKES IN NATURE

Long ago in the Earth's history there was an age of reptiles, an age which lasted for perhaps 100 million years. Reptiles grew to amazing sizes; some were as much as 80 ft. long while one may have reached the staggering weight of 50 tons! Those giants have all disappeared long since, but reptiles have survived by developing into very different shapes, and they are now on the small rather than the large side. The reptiles, one of the classes of Vertebrate (back-boned) animals, vary greatly in shape, size and habits, but they all have the following characteristics in common:

1. Body normally covered with hard, dry skin which is divided clearly into scales or shields; for each kind these form a more or less fixed pattern, even though the colours may vary.
2. Lungs, by means of which they breathe air even though they may live in water.
3. No body temperature regulation; that is, reptiles do not have a constant temperature, like birds and mammals, but usually vary with their surroundings.
4. Internal fertilisation of eggs, as in birds and mammals. Most reptiles lay eggs whose shells are either leathery (snakes and lizards) or hard (crocodiles), but in some snakes and lizards the eggs are retained inside the body of the female until they hatch.
5. Young which closely resemble the adults and are independent of them as soon as they are hatched.

Living reptiles fall into five easily recognised groups. The order *Chelonia* includes the turtles, terrapins and tortoises, with nearly 250 kinds. The order *Rhynchocephalia* consists only of the rare Tuatara from New Zealand, nearest in relationship to many of the ancient reptiles. The order *Loricata* is made up of the crocodiles and their relations, numbering some two dozen kinds. The order *Squamata* is divided into the *Lacertilia* (lizards), with over 2,000 species, and the *Ophidia* (snakes), with over 1,700 species.

Being without legs, a snake can hardly be mistaken for a typical lizard, but some lizards also are legless and it is not at all easy to describe in simple language just how to distinguish the border-line lizards and snakes. Lizards usually have movable eyelids, while in snakes these are fixed over the eye and are transparent, but in some lizards and snakes the eyes have almost disappeared, so this feature does not always help. In snakes the two parts of the lower jaw are joined in front by an elastic ligament and fastened only loosely to the upper jaw; in lizards the two parts of the lower jaw are fused or more tightly joined together, and this is hinged firmly to the upper jaw. This, however, is not a feature likely to help a beginner in the field.

In typical snakes the under-surface is covered with long, transverse scales running almost the width of the body, each fastened to a pair of ribs; in lizards the scales are more or less the same size all round the body, but the burrowing Worm Snakes and the Blind Snakes are exceptions to this general rule.

Snakes and lizards shed the dead outer layer of skin at varying intervals, the snakes generally in one piece, the lizards always in small pieces: this is known as sloughing. The result is the replacement of a dull and perhaps damaged surface by a new and slightly larger one.

Snakes and lizards are the most successful reptile groups today, and they are found in almost every part of the world except the true deserts and the permanently frozen north and

SNAKES IN NATURE

south. Only one kind of lizard is marine, but one complete family of snakes, the sea snakes, lives only in the sea and is very numerous in the Pacific and the South Seas. Some snakes are tree-dwellers and spend the greater part of their life off the ground. Others are specialised burrowers and seldom come to the surface unless driven out of their tunnels by flooding. Some, like the giant vipers, are so heavy that they cannot climb far, but many, like the Black Cobra and the Green Mamba, are equally at home on the ground or in trees. Some snakes live and feed in streams and lakes, and all can swim. With more than a hundred kinds, West Africa has representatives of all the important groups, except the sea snakes and the rattlesnake family. Although a striped sea eel is sometimes mistaken for a snake, there are quite certainly no sea snakes on the West African coast and the only reptiles found in the sea are the turtles.

Snakes take only animal food, and their teeth and jaws are such that it must be swallowed whole. (Poison teeth—fangs—will be mentioned in detail later.) All snakes have sharp, solid teeth, generally numerous, with which the prey is seized. These teeth point slightly backwards and also serve to push the food down into the throat, but they cannot chew the food or tear it to pieces; their stomachs digest everything except hair, hoof, horn and teeth. Most snakes drink a good deal of water.

Some snakes are specialised feeders: for instance, the Royal Python usually takes only a few kinds of mice, perhaps only one kind. The Black Cobra is just the reverse, eating mammals, birds and their eggs, lizards, toads and fish. The smallest snakes of all—the Worm Snakes—feed on the eggs and small larvae (young forms) of insects, especially ants; the young of many of the smaller snakes probably feed at first on insects.

There is usually no obvious difference between male and female, but for any one kind the female's tail is always comparatively shorter. The female usually grows to a greater total length.

Pairing occurs after a varying amount of courtship ceremony. One fertilisation by the male may serve several batches of eggs laid over a period of several months. Snakes' eggs are usually laid among moist vegetation or soil, and then left to hatch without any further attention; but the pythons incubate their eggs, and it seems that cobras and mambas may do this or guard the place where they have left theirs. In snakes like the Gaboon Viper that bear living young, the eggs hatch within the mother's body, and they generally emerge in one big batch.

Most snakes other than burrowing kinds have adequate sight, though their eyes are very different in structure from lizards' eyes. Snakes are practically deaf, but they may "hear" by feeling vibrations through their lower jaws. Although snakes cannot "smell" as mammals can, they have a sense organ in the snout known as "Organ of Jacobson", with which they can "smell". The tongue, with its forked tip, conveys tiny scent particles to this organ, which can best be described as combining the senses of both scent and taste. A few snakes, including the rattlesnakes (known as pit-vipers) and pythons, have small pits on the face or around the margins of the jaw; these pits are well supplied with tiny nerves and can detect warmth, thus enabling the snake to find warm-blooded creatures in the dark.

Snakes move in several different ways, but the most usual is an undulatory movement; the muscles on either side of the body work alternately, thrusting forward first one side and then the other, but doing this so rapidly and smoothly that it appears to be one continuous gliding movement. Heavy-bodied, slow-moving snakes, like the giant vipers, can move in a more or less straight line by stretching and contracting alternately, rather as a worm moves, but using the large ventral scales to get a grip. Desert snakes, such as the Horned Viper and the Desert Rattlesnakes, have developed a type of movement ideal for travelling on sandy surfaces which are too loose to give a firm grip. The body is thrown half forward, half sideways, in a series of loops known as "side-winding", and leaves tracks in the form of a series of diagonal lines.

The speed of snakes is much misunderstood. One reason for this is that it is most difficult to judge the speed of an animal moving in a strange or unfamiliar way—which is how it appears to us. Another factor is that snakes are seldom regarded just as ordinary animals; people tend to regard them as dangerous, poisonous, aggressive and terrifying, and assume that they can go much faster than is really the case. The fastest snakes travel at between 5 and 6 m.p.h. and many kinds, including the giant vipers, can scarcely reach 1 m.p.h. These figures do not apply to the "strike"; from a coiled position on the alert, a snake can strike very rapidly and accurately for a distance amounting to perhaps half its own length.

To the newcomer interested in snakes the first problem is to identify the different kinds, and, especially, to recognise those that are dangerous. In a country like England the problem hardly exists, for there are only three kinds of snake and one snake-like lizard. In Ghana, however, there are over 80 different snakes, and in Nigeria even more. Some are common, some are rare; some are widespread and some live in only a few localities; while some can be identified at a glance, others are very hard indeed to name, even when seen clearly and examined in the hand.

A book of this length can deal only with the more important and common snakes and those that are quite easily identified. The minimum of technical terms is used, and I hope that from the information given here, in both text and illustrations, the reader can put names to most snakes likely to show themselves, or at least recognise their group. There is no short cut to knowing all the snakes, and it is not even possible, as with birds, to name fairly quickly the family to which a snake belongs. The identity of many snakes can be discovered only with the use of a lens to check the smaller details, but unless the snake is quite certainly harmless, it is most unwise for beginners to handle live snakes.

The first point to realise is that colour does not always help. Green Mambas are always green and the Gaboon and Rhinoceros Vipers always have their fantastic "jazz" patterns of colours, but the cobras and Hissing Sand Snakes may have four or five different colours or patterns, even within the same area, and the Blanding's Tree Snake can be either black or brown! Even snakes whose colours are usually fairly constant may occasionally appear in a black (melanistic) form, as happens with many other animals, especially in the carnivorous mammals. I was several times deceived by a rare black form of a common green tree snake which looked remarkably like a young Black Cobra.

It is hoped that many readers of this little book will not be content with identifying just the more important snakes, but will want to name any snake they come across. Identification of the family is the first step, and the important feature here is the presence or absence of fangs, the hollow teeth through which venom is discharged. By careful examination of the mouth we can divide snakes into the following four types:

1. With erect fangs in the very front of the upper jaw (the cobra/mamba family) (Fig. 1a).
2. With curved fangs hinged in front of the upper jaw and folding up and back along the roof of the mouth (vipers) (Fig. 1b).
3. With one or two fangs towards the back of the rows of teeth on either side of the upper jaw (back-fanged snakes) (Fig. 1c).
4. With no fangs at all (Fig. 1d).

(The sea snakes and pit-vipers, which are not found in West Africa, belong to the first and second types respectively.) Even though the snake may be dead, use the greatest care when

SNAKES IN NATURE

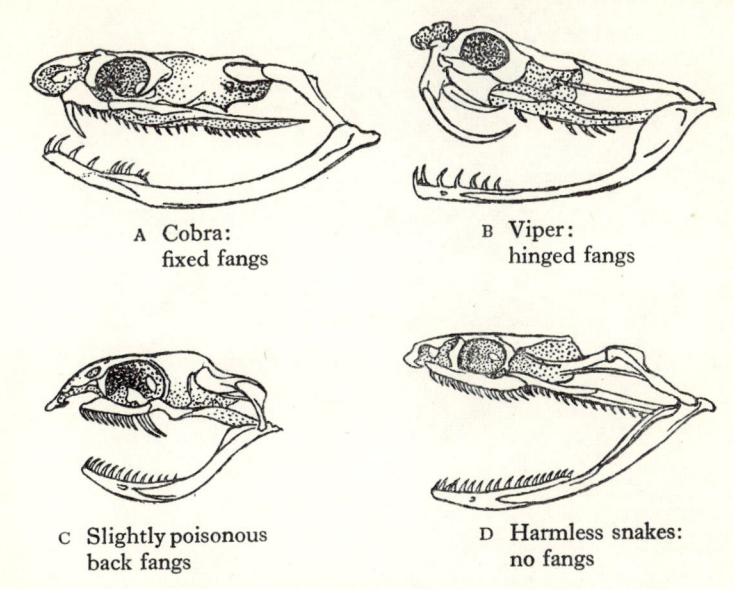

A Cobra:
fixed fangs

B Viper:
hinged fangs

C Slightly poisonous
back fangs

D Harmless snakes:
no fangs

FIG. 1.—PROFILE OF SNAKES' SKULLS

examining the teeth and never touch them with a bare finger; the teeth stay sharp and the snake's venom remains potent long after death.

Museum folk are concerned with the snake's internal anatomy, but the field naturalist must depend largely on the scales, which completely cover every snake and which have the same number and pattern for the whole of the snake's life, even though their colour may and often does change. Each group of scales has its own name, e.g. the ventral scales along the belly, the sub-caudal scales underneath the tail, the labials along the lips, and so on. Their names are generally self-explanatory and easily understood by anyone really interested, even though they may know nothing very technical about snakes (see Fig. 2).

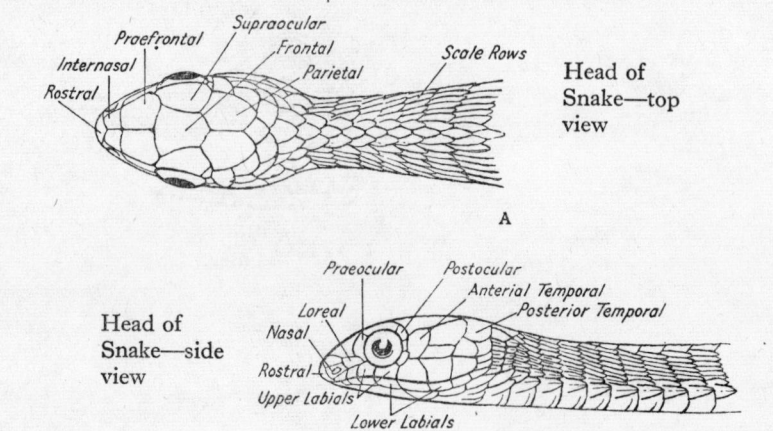

WEST AFRICAN SNAKES

A — Head of Snake—top view. Labels: Rostral, Internasal, Praefrontal, Supraocular, Frontal, Parietal, Scale Rows.

B — Head of Snake—side view. Labels: Praeocular, Postocular, Anterior Temporal, Posterior Temporal, Loreal, Nasal, Rostral, Upper Labials, Lower Labials.

C — Labels: Vertebral Scales, Dorsal and Lateral Scales, Ventral Scales.

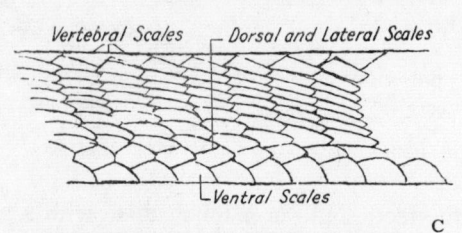

Side view of centre of body showing scale count. Nine rows of scales on one side including the vertebral scale. This makes a total of 19 rows. The broad ventral plate is not counted

D — Under-side view of tail end showing scale details. Labels: Ventral, Subcaudal-Single, Anal-Divided, Subcaudal-Paired.

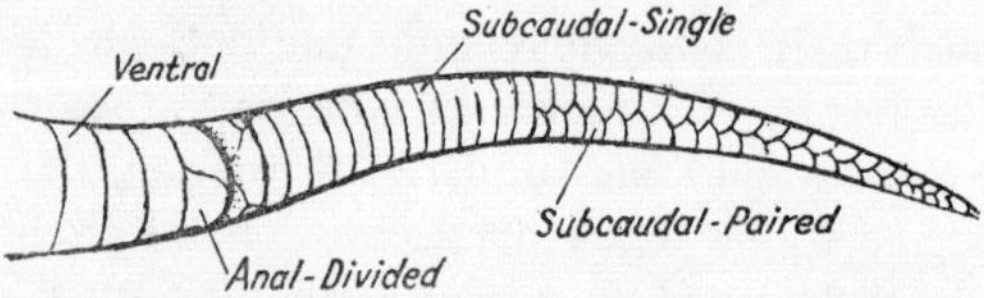

FIG. 2.—SCALE PATTERNS AND NAMES

Snake scales can vary in type (whether smooth and shiny as in the Black Cobra, or keeled and rough as in the giant vipers); and in size, shape and number. In addition, the presence or absence of some of these scales, especially on the face, may be of importance. The ratio of tail to total length may also help in identification.

All this is very much less complicated than it might sound and in a book such as Villiers's* the keys are arranged as a series of simple alternatives, taking just one feature at a time. One does not need a scientific training to be able to use them.

CHAPTER II

SNAKES IN WEST AFRICA: FREQUENCY, SOCIAL AND ECONOMIC IMPORTANCE

No part of West Africa is without snakes, though their numbers and kinds vary very much and no two areas have exactly the same list. It is generally true that the more luxuriant the vegetation, the greater the variety of wild life to be found; so we find the widest range of species in the tropical forests and the shortest lists in the dry semi-desert around the Sahara. Little has been recorded about West African snakes: most kinds have

*Villiers, A. (1950), *Les Serpents de l'Ouest Africain* (Dakar I.F.A.N.).

probably been named and described by now, but we have much to learn about their distribution and we know hardly anything about their numbers. One gets the impression that snakes, like many other smaller animals, become much more common in old farmlands and around the farms and village clearings. This seems reasonable enough, because it is obvious that plenty of food is available for the mice, rats, squirrels, etc., on which they prey, but it could be that snakes only *seem* more plentiful because they are more easily seen in such places. In the dense jungle every possible niche is occupied; there are snakes in the trees which we seldom or never see, and perhaps a dozen other kinds that live underground and are found only by accident. Those living in trees are found nowhere else, but some underground species are less particular and they may also make their home in the soil of the open grass country, which occurs around, and mostly to the north of, the high forest or jungle.

Similarly the water snakes, at any rate the common one known as Smyth's Water Snake, can live in fresh water almost anywhere. Most snakes at home in or on the dry sandy soils—as, for instance, the Sand Boa and some of the vipers—cannot live in different conditions, but some open country snakes are more adaptable and have occupied the big forest clearings, following their favourite prey which had already moved in. Good examples of this class are the Night Adder, which feeds on the Common Toad, and the African Beauty Snake (*Psammophis*), preying on gerbils and small lizards.

The longest and largest snake in West Africa—the African Python—is also the most widespread; in fact it is found in suitable places, generally near water, in most of Africa south of the Sahara. An Ivory Coast record of 32 ft. 8 in. shows that this python challenges the Reticulated Python of Malaya (and possibly the Anaconda of Brazil) in the claim to be the world's longest snake. Some of the world's smallest snakes are also

SNAKES IN WEST AFRICA

found in West Africa—tiny blind Worm Snakes no thicker than the lead in a pencil and only 5 or 6 in. long.

In most parts of West Africa the average townsman hardly knows the names of even the commonest snakes. Little has been written about the names of snakes in other West African countries, and on this point I speak personally only about Ghana, where I found the dangerous snakes generally well known by name to the country folk, and recognised for what they were; if any confusion occurred it was that somewhat similar, but harmless, snakes were included with the dangerous ones, in both name and reputation. The really conspicuous snakes generally had their own names, as for instance, Smyth's Water Snake and the Red-lined Snake, but in the open country of the coastal regions the numerous striped snakes seemed to have no very definite name; perhaps this was because I was working mostly with labourers and others who were not natives of the area. As in mammals, another general rule seems to be that the rather small snakes (say, under 3 ft.) which are neither dangerous, conspicuous nor edible are seldom recognised as other than just "snakes". Curious groupings may be found. For instance the Burrowing Boa (*Calabaria*) is called by the same name as the Spotted Blind Snake, because of their common subterranean habit; the Blanding's Tree Snake (back-fanged) and the Egg-eating Snake (harmless) are utterly unlike and yet have the same name because they are both said to eat eggs. The two giant vipers of the forest zone (Gaboon and Rhinoceros) have completely different colours and patterns, yet if ever they are distinguished by name it is merely to refer to the Rhinoceros Viper as the "Black ɔnanka"; farmers, the people most familiar with them, seldom separated them. With a few important exceptions, therefore, native names are not much more use than colours in identifying unknown snakes.

There will always be argument about the deadliness of snakes, but West Africa has at least 10 kinds whose bites may easily prove fatal to a human being. These include the Gaboon Viper, Carpet Viper, Green Mambas and Black Cobras, which must be reckoned among the most poisonous snakes in the world.

The last chapter deals with snake bite and its treatment, but I think it should be stressed here that to a person going about his everyday life in and around a town, snakes are much less a danger to life than the bicycle or car on which he rides to work. Those working in the farms and forests obviously run a much greater risk, especially if they are working bare-footed, because the great majority of bites are received on the lower legs and feet; shoes and boots and any kind of leg covering greatly reduce the chances of being seriously bitten. It seems, from figures collected by Father Lesage, that deaths from snake bite in Ghana may amount to a hundred in a year, mostly in distant places far from medical help. This figure may seem rather frightening, but it must be remembered that Ghana is some 85,000 square miles in extent, with a population of some 5 million.

I spent 14 years in the Forestry Department of Ghana. The Department had staff numbering many hundreds working in all parts of the forest, and in that time no member of the staff died of snake bite and I knew only of two colleagues being bitten. Here is another figure which may also be of interest. In 4 years of field-training during the war, involving tens of thousands of soldiers on day and night exercises in the bush, only 3 cases of death from snake bite were recorded. The average person in West Africa is much more likely to die in a road accident than from snake bite!

By most West Africans and many Europeans, nearly all snakes are regarded as deadly poisonous and to be killed or avoided at all costs. This is probably a sound general policy, but it does not encourage people to learn much about snakes. Some forest people recognise the Blind Snake (*Typhlops*) as harmless, but these and pythons seem to be almost the only exceptions. Many Africans believe firmly that snakes have a sting at the

SNAKES IN WEST AFRICA

end of the tail as well as poison teeth. In some kinds the tail may end in a distinct point, but this tip is solid and has no poison of any kind.

In some parts of West Africa, especially in the coastal regions and along the rivers, the python is considered a sacred animal. Some tribes regard it as the spirit of the rivers, others as the god of war, the goddess of fertility, of wisdom and so on. In Dahomey it has long been the custom to keep a python in special quarters where it is fed and cared for by the fetish priests and priestesses. It was presumably a representation of a python that I saw at fetish shrines in the Keta area from time to time when I was working there, but I found the people unwilling to say very much about them.

In a number of places, too, the snake is, or once was, associated with the rainbow and credited with powers of controlling the rainfall and the rivers. There is also a widespread belief that after death a person can become reincarnated as a snake of various kinds. An old woman died of snake bite in a North Ashanti village that I was once visiting. When I told the chief that had he let me know I could have treated her, he replied that I could have done nothing at all because it was actually her late departed uncle who had returned in snake form for the purpose of killing this woman!

Groups of snake-charmers perform in the market places of Nigeria and Ghana, while in parts of Sierra Leone they seem to have a place in some local religious festivities. Black Cobras or Spitting Cobras are most frequently used in these blood-curdling exhibitions, and, as far as I know, it is not yet fully clear why the charmers are seldom fatally bitten. It may be true that many of the cobras have lost their teeth by being provoked into biting at a piece of cloth which is then jerked rapidly, but these poison fangs can be replaced within a comparatively few days. Fatal bites are reported from time to time, showing that at least some of these snakes have not been rendered completely harmless. It is also true that many cobras soon settle down and become docile, seldom bothering to spread their hoods or strike even when provoked, and this may be the explanation. I always found Green Mambas to have a very different temperament and one never hears of these being used for snake-charming.

We do not know enough about West African snakes to speak of their economic importance. As a cause of death to humans and livestock they are almost negligible, but on and around village and town clearings snakes kill many small animals such as mice and squirrels which often damage crops and food stores. Even the Black Cobra kills and eats the Black Rat and therefore does good. On the other hand, pythons and the giant vipers feed largely on mammals and birds that would otherwise be suitable for human food, but they in turn are eaten by certain tribal groups.

Like most animals living in the tropics, snakes have many enemies, and the effectiveness of these enemies is suggested by the large families that the snakes often produce. The giant vipers may have as many as 60 young ones at a time, the African Python up to 100, and yet they never become very common, and on the average less than one out of each batch of eggs or young is likely to reach full size.

Mongooses, civets and wild pigs are perhaps the most important enemies among the mammals. The Honey Badger probably eats small snakes, and hedgehogs and shrews are likely to attack the very small species or young snakes a few inches long.

Many birds include snakes in their diet and several of the day birds of prey take little else. Only two specimens of the Gold Coast Serpent Eagle have been collected recently: one had just eaten 2 small Black Cobras and 1 Green Mamba, while the other contained a Green Mamba, so it looks as if this bird prefers poisonous snakes. The Secretary Bird of the

SNAKES IN WEST AFRICA

grass country is well known as an expert catcher of snakes, trampling on them with its long bare legs and using a wing as a shield. The Ground Hornbill is equally effective and even the Tree Hornbills attack snakes greedily, as well as lizards, although their main food is a variety of tree fruits. Cattle Egrets and other members of the heron tribe that hunt their food away from the water also snap up any small snakes they come across and swallow them whole.

Several snakes are wholly or partly cannibal, but the only other important reptile enemies are Monitor Lizards; these are almost omnivorous and though they may not concentrate on snakes, they are likely to eat many snakes and their eggs.

Driver Ants are a menace to almost all forms of life and even large snakes are not always able to get away. On two occasions I happened on snakes of 2 to 3 ft. in length nearly covered with ants and quite unable to escape. In the rainy season these ants are likely to be the snake's most serious enemy. It is firmly believed by many Ashanti hunters that after killing a large animal, but before swallowing it, a python makes a long circuit through the forest in order to make sure that there are no driver ants about that might attack it while digesting its meal and therefore hardly able to move.

Man is also an enemy, killing any snake within range, but it is by setting fire to farms and, more especially, the dry grasslands that he does most damage. These fires sweep across the country at great speed and drive everything living before them, exposing them to attack by birds and other enemies, as well as claiming many direct victims. Fire is probably the snake's most serious single enemy in the long dry season.

Many West African groups, though not all, kill pythons and giant vipers for food. The meat is said to be very good eating.

CHAPTER III

THE PYTHON FAMILY

The Python/Boa family is found in most parts of the tropics. With only two exceptions (the King Cobra and the Black Mamba) all snakes of 12 ft. or more in length are pythons or boas, but not all kinds are giants: some pythons and boas are only 4 to 5 ft. long and several are even smaller than that.

1. The African or Rock Python (*Plate I*)
Python sebae

The African Python or Rock Python is Africa's only large python. It produces the familiar python skins and it is almost the only snake that is so well known as not to need description. Its pattern is hard to describe simply and it is much better illustrated; brown is the predominant colour, varying from very pale to a brown so dark that it is almost black. The pattern on the head itself is fairly constant, with a rough arrow in dark brown, surrounded by a very pale margin, nearly covering the top of the head. The Royal Python has similar colours, but its pattern is always much more clear-cut and it is stouter, length for length.

There will always be arguments about the size of big snakes. African Pythons 10 ft. long are quite common; specimens up to 15 ft. are not very rare, but a python of over 20 ft. is distinctly unusual. On two occasions farmers in my area killed pythons that were probably close to 20 ft. long, though certainly not more than that. A mining engineer working in north-west Ashanti told me of one that he had shot measuring about 24 ft. in length; this was the largest of which I had personal

THE PYTHON FAMILY

knowledge, but I have no doubt that larger pythons exist in all West African territories. I can find few reports of giant pythons from other parts of West Africa, but there is an authentic record of a 32 ft. 8 in. specimen from Bingerville in the Ivory Coast in 1932. This seems to be by far the longest yet found anywhere in Africa.

The weight of a snake varies according to its condition and stomach content. For instance, Pitman records one of 14 ft. which weighed 135 lb., having just eaten a Bushbuck. On the other hand another measured over 15 ft. but weighed only 60 lb. The weight is obviously greater if the body is full of eggs.

This python is found through much of Africa south of the Sahara, including the whole of West Africa. Unlike many snakes and other animals, it is found in both closed forest and grassland, generally not far from water and often actually in it.

A number of the pythons which I collected in Ghana had been found by fishermen in fishtraps set under water, but it is hard to suggest why they should enter these traps, for they are not known to eat cold-blooded prey such as fish. They can survive for several hours under water without breathing: there is obviously a limit to the time they can stay submerged, but I did not hear of many being found dead. Perhaps the fishermen just threw them away and did not bother to inform me.

The African Python is most active in the evening and at night, and this probably explains why it is seldom seen on the move. It is equally at home on the ground or in trees and is an expert swimmer.

Pythons lay eggs, and they are among the very few kinds of snake that incubate their eggs, the female coiling her body around them to protect them and to keep them warm. This has now been studied in a zoo and it has been found that the snake's body has a temperature about 14°F. higher than the air around it; for instance, where the cage temperature was 72°F., the snake's own temperature was 86°F. This contradicts the general rule that reptiles have the temperature of their surroundings, and it is probably explained by the twitching of the female's body, which generates heat in the same way as our skin muscles when we shiver. Python eggs have a soft, leathery shell and are about 3 in. in diameter, but they soon lose their round shape as the female presses around them. About 40 eggs is a normal clutch for a female of 14 or 15 ft., but there may be as many as 100. The young hatch after about 6–8 weeks and are some 20–22 in. long; they are thinner than one's little finger and weigh about 3 oz. They grow at varying rates dependent on the conditions around them; if these are favourable they may reach 6 ft. in the first year, but if suitable food is hard to find, growth is much slower. The young have a similar pattern to that found in older snakes, but it is less clearly defined and the colours are rather duller.

The larger the python, the bigger is the prey that it can swallow, but this does not mean that large pythons eat only large animals. In captivity, for instance, pythons over 20 ft. long may be fed on rabbits, pigeons and chickens, though they can kill and swallow animals as large as a Bushbuck and weighing at least 1 cwt. African Pythons are said to eat frogs and toads when very hungry, but mammals and birds are their usual food. They cannot move fast enough to pursue active prey and must generally wait for it to come within range, the colour and pattern of their skin allowing them to remain unrecognised. With a very swift movement the head shoots out and the mouth grips the victim; two or three turns of the python's body then wrap around it, particularly around the chest; if the victim is strong and large the python will put further coils around it to subdue it. The victim is killed by asphyxiation (i.e. prevented from breathing), and not by crushing, as is often stated. I have never known a python to start eating its prey until it is quite dead, and it is rare for it to be swallowed other than head first.

Plate I

2. Royal Python

1. African Python or Rock Python

Plate II

4. Sand Boa
3. Calabar Ground Python

Plate III

6. Red-lined Snake   5. Spotted Blind Snake

Plate IV

7.

8.

7. Smyth's Water Snake
8. The Fierce Snake

THE PYTHON FAMILY

Pythons occasionally swallow porcupines. In 1948 the Dublin Zoo received an African Python 12 ft. long which had been in captivity for three months. A year after arrival it passed several long quills among its droppings, showing that it had swallowed a porcupine over 15 months earlier. Quills are made of the same substance as hair and therefore are not dissolved by the stomach juices. Pythons can live for long periods without food: some authorities say that a fast may be as long as 3 years and one of 6 months is not uncommon.

Although a very large python would be strong enough to kill a man, such a happening is very unlikely and in the whole of Africa there do not seem to be more than two or three cases of humans being killed and swallowed. This may be partly because a human body, with its broad shoulders, is a very difficult shape to swallow, but like most other snakes, pythons normally try to escape from men, and the person most likely to be hurt is the one who tries to capture a python. An experienced snake-catcher can safely tackle one of at least 10 ft., but for any python larger than that he needs assistance, and it is wise to have one person for every 4 or 5 ft. of snake!

2. The Royal Python *(Plate I)*

Python regius

The Royal Python is quite clearly a python, but it can hardly be confused with the much larger Rock Python. Its name comes from the handsome and clear-cut markings, but it is also called the Ball Python or, in Sierra Leone, the "shame snake", because it rolls into a tight ball, hiding its head in the middle: this habit is not seen so much in snakes that have been handled a lot. The general background colour is a dark brown and there are a number of much paler irregular lengthwise patches, with one or more darker centres. The neck always narrows abruptly immediately behind the head, whereas in the larger python the neck is nearly as broad as the head. In the centre of the body it is normally at least twice as thick as an African Python of the same length.

Royal Pythons never reach a very large size. Over most of their range they seldom exceed 4 ft., while 5 ft. would be considered the maximum, but in some areas, especially along the slopes of the Krobo Hills behind Accra, they may grow distinctly bigger. Specimens of 6 ft. in length are not unusual and even larger ones have been found.

This python is a snake of the open forest and grasslands of West and Central Africa and it is found from Senegal in the west through to the Sudan and Uganda in the east, including all the West African countries. It cannot live in closed forest, but it has colonised the grasslands around Freetown which have resulted from heavy clearing and farming.

In many parts of its range its main food seems to be one of the jumping mice or Gerbils; these are active at night and the Royal Python presumably hunts them then, but it is sometimes caught while sunning itself in the open during the daytime. It is perhaps because it is used to preying mostly on one kind of animal that this snake is usually so slow to start feeding in captivity. Two caught near Accra spent 22 months in a British Zoo before their first feed, but after that they took mice freely. One that I kept in London refused all food for over 14 months and then killed and swallowed a white rat.

The Royal Python makes a pleasant pet and can be freely handled; only one in many that I have owned over the past 20 years has been vicious, and this was most aggressive for several weeks, even striking at the glass of its cage. Then it settled down happily and was no trouble at all.

Little seems to be known about the breeding of this little python except that it incubates its eggs. One would expect it to lay many fewer eggs than the large kind.

THE PYTHON FAMILY

The two remaining West African members of the python family are burrowing snakes which grow to a much smaller size than those already discussed and less is known about them. They are seldom seen and are found only by accident, but both are easy to recognise.

3. The Calabar Ground Python *(Plate II)*
Calabaria reinhardtii

The Burrowing Boa, better called the Calabar Ground Python, is a snake of the forest zone and ranges from Liberia in the west to the Ituri forest of the Congo in the east. It usually has the same native name as the Blind Snakes, but is easily distinguished from them by having the usual broad ventral plates across the under surface; in the Blind Snakes tiny, highly polished scales run right around the body and there are no ventral plates. As in most burrowing snakes, the body has more or less the same diameter throughout and the head and tail ends are roughly the same thickness. The general colour is a warm reddish-brown, with a few lighter spots which give it a speckled appearance. The colour seems constant and it does not vary with age. Most adult specimens are between 2 and 3 ft. long, but my best, taken at Oda, Ghana, was 41 in. long, which seems considerably longer than any previously recorded.

Although it has been suggested that the Ground Python spends most of its time in mouse holes and feeds on small rodents, it is hard to see how a constricting snake could deal with them there. I took over a dozen specimens, most of which were caught alive and at once sent to zoos, where they proved almost impossible to feed. Only one showed any interest in a small mouse, which it constricted but did not eat, while another used to swallow large worms after the end had been placed inside the mouth. The few that had been killed before arrival were examined carefully and no identifiable food remains were ever found in the stomach, which suggests that worms might possibly be their food, rather than mice or other small mammals, but this would be strange food for one of the python family.

Perhaps someone reading this book may have the opportunity to study this problem in the field and solve the mystery.

The Ground Python is very gentle and inoffensive, and it has a habit of rolling itself into a defensive ball, though this is not generally so round and tight as in the Royal Python. It belongs to the python section of the Python/Boa family and lays eggs, though probably only a small number in each batch.

4. The Sand Boa (Plate II)
Eryx muelleri

The Sand Boa is found in very different country, for it is a snake of the desert edge, specialised for living in sandy soil, and it extends only into the driest parts of West Africa. Its exact range is still unknown: it seems to be absent from the dry coastal belt of Ghana and Dahomey, but it is found in the northern part of Ghana and in much of the Northern Provinces of Nigeria. Three different forms of Sand Boa are found, but only one of these probably comes within any of the British Commonwealth countries. The two others are found around the edge of the Sahara, from Mauritania in the west to Egypt in the east.

The Sand Boa is well fitted for life in the sand. Its snout is wedge-shaped, for pushing down below the surface; the body is more or less the same thickness from the head to the very short tail, which ends in a blunt point and is therefore much feared by the local people. The colour is a pale yellow or orange, with irregular brownish patches of varying size. The scales are small and numerous, being in about 40 rows around the middle of the body; they are also quite smooth, and this character, with the small head, which is not at all distinct from the body, makes the Sand Boa easily distinguished from the very venomous sand-living vipers. Some reach a length of up to 30 in., though Mueller's Sand Boa, the one most likely to be met, reaches only 20 in.

The ground surface temperature in most parts of the Sand Boa's range would be too high for it to be exposed by day for any period and it usually protects itself from the direct sun by hiding under a layer of sand or soil. At night it lies half buried in the surface and presumably depends on its camouflage to let its prey come within striking range, for it is slow and sluggish and could not pursue such active prey as tiny quails and other birds on which it has been known to feed. Its main victims are small Gerbils and Jerboas, which it kills by constriction. In the less sandy areas it also lives in the shallow tunnels of the Gerbils.

In contrast to the gentle Ground Pythons, some Sand Boas are vicious and aggressive; they do not strike in the normal manner, but by rapid head movements make a series of slashes in the skin of an unwary hand and these may bleed profusely. The Sand Boa is also able to defend itself by releasing a foul-smelling substance from its vent, as often happens in the English Grass Snake. This snake is a typical boa in its breeding habits, bearing living young, probably in rather small batches. The East African Sand Boa, which reaches as far as the French Niger Territory, is recorded as having 7 young at a time.

CHAPTER IV

HARMLESS SNAKES

Most snakes are without poison teeth of any kind. West Africa has a bewildering assortment of these harmless snakes and many of them are not easy to identify exactly; while, on the contrary, most of the really dangerous ones can be recognised at a glance. There is no easy way of knowing that a snake is harmless, except the general rule that any snakes having big heads and thick in proportion to their length are very poisonous; that any green snakes over 4 ft. long in the forest zone are almost certainly Green Mambas, and that any smooth all black snake over 6 ft. long is most probably a cobra. When in any doubt, assume that a snake is poisonous and examine it very cautiously.

The pythons, belonging to a separate family and easily recognised at a glance, are, of course, entirely non-poisonous, but they are described in Chapter III. Most harmless snakes form one part of the *Colubridae*, a world-wide family of snakes, but before attempting to sort them out we must deal with two small families of burrowing snakes which are seldom seen and virtually impossible to keep successfully in captivity.

These two families are quite easily recognised, for they have a feature which distinguishes them from all other snakes; the ventral scales have exactly the same shape as those on the flanks and the upper surface, whereas the typical snakes have transverse ventral plates much longer than wide.

THE WORM SNAKES

Leptotyphlopidae

Members of one of these small families, known to zoologists as the *Leptotyphlopidae* and to naturalists as Worm Snakes, are seldom recognised as snakes. They are very small, measuring only 5–7 in. when fully grown, and with a body about as thick as a pencil lead. The mouth is minute, with some very small solid teeth, in the lower jaw only, and these Worm Snakes feed entirely on tiny insects, especially ants and their eggs. Some

HARMLESS SNAKES

8 different species are found in various parts of West Africa, mostly in the dry country outside the high forest, but they have been collected so seldom that their habits and distribution are still little known.

The colour of these tiny Worm Snakes varies from pale brown to blackish. The scales are always rather smooth, shiny and dry, distinguishing them at a glance from worms; examined under a lens, they are seen to have no more than 14 rows of scales around the body. The eyes are scarcely or not at all visible, and the body is of more or less the same thickness throughout its length. Worm Snakes seldom come above ground on their own and are usually found purely by chance. The only specimens I received were found by small children while hoeing their farm plots.

THE BLIND SNAKES OR GLASS SNAKES

Typhlopidae

Members of the *Typhlops* family are much larger and better known. They have tiny teeth on the upper jaw, but none, or perhaps one only each side, on the lower. In common with the Ground Python they are known in many parts as "double-ended" snakes, and the Ashanti name (nitinifro) means, literally, "they haven't a head and they haven't a tail", i.e. it is impossible to tell one end from the other. In Ghana many farmers recognise this Spotted Blind Snake as harmless, but in some parts of West Africa and also in East Africa it is regarded as more than usually poisonous. Six species of *Typhlops* are known in West Africa and they are generally either brown or yellow-brown; one or more are recorded as sometimes being blackish, when they might possibly be confused with the most unpleasant Burrowing Vipers, and this could account for their being branded as deadly.

The smallest reaches about 10 in. and the largest over 30 in. in length, and their much greater size means that they are noticed more frequently. They are also of heavier build, the small ones being some ¼ in. thick and the largest at least an inch. They are like the Worm Snakes in many ways and also feed on tiny insects underground.

In the West African forest zone the Blind Snakes are not often found in farming operations; this may be because the digging is not deep enough, but it is also thought that these snakes prefer living near or among the roots of trees. In areas where pit-sawing takes place it is worth searching old saw-pits in the rainy season for any that have been flooded out of their tunnels. I have seen as many as six of them swimming around in a pit half-full of water. Other snakes are also trapped in this way, but most of the active varieties, with large ventral scales, can climb up the rough sides of the pit and escape.

5. The Spotted Blind Snake *(Plate III)*
Typhlops punctatus

It is not easy to distinguish the 6 different species recorded for West Africa. The commonest of them, known best as the Spotted Blind Snake, is also by far the largest, reaching at least 30 in. The others are much smaller—less than 15 in. long. The Spotted Blind Snake's colour varies, but is generally brown, more or less spotted or marbled with paler brown or yellow, and the skin always has a glassy polish.

COLUBRIDAE

The majority of harmless snakes belong to a part of the *Colubridae* family, the most widespread and numerous snakes in the world. They are usually slender-bodied, of small to medium size, and most do not exceed 6 ft. in length. With a few exceptions, probably none of them in West Africa, they lay eggs. Something like 40 species are so far recorded for West Africa, and it is hard to know where to start, for even experienced naturalists have difficulty in putting names to some of the smaller ones, and the differences between even some of the larger and more distinct species are not always obvious.

6. The Red-lined Snake *(Plate III)*
Bothropthalmus lineatus

Of those which are recognisable at a glance, even to a beginner, the most outstanding is the Red-lined Snake of the forest country. It likes moist places and it is often seen near or actually in forest streams. It sometimes reaches a length of 4 ft. and is of average stoutness, a 4-ft. specimen being under 1 in. thick. The under-surface is bright red; the upper parts are black with one narrow red line along the backbone and two narrow lines along each side. In young specimens up to 12 in. or so the head is white, but otherwise this species is remarkably constant in colouring. When first caught it is usually active and rather vicious, but it settles down quickly and stops striking. The Red-lined Snake feeds on small mammals, especially on mice and shrews.

7. Smyth's Water Snake *(Plate IV)*
Grayia smythii

Several other snakes are also water-loving and two can fairly be described as water snakes. Smyth's Water Snake is a most handsome species but as liable to colour variation as almost any other snake in the whole area. It may be found in waters of all sizes, from large rivers and lakes down to tiny forest streams and pools, and sometimes is extremely common. In a tiny deep pool near my headquarters at Akim Oda we could always see half a dozen or more of them, but they were so expert at hiding among the tree roots that we could never catch them.

In Ghana, and presumably in other parts of the area, four main colour forms are found; two are more or less uniform, either dark slatey-grey or brown; the other two are these same colours with a series of narrow pale bands at more or less regular intervals along the body. The underside is always very pale, sometimes almost white, with a series of small black patches where the underside joins the darker sides; the mouth has a black and white pattern and the throat is usually a rich yellow. Smyth's Water Snake is rather stout for its length, being over 1 in. thick at 4 ft. in length and there is no distinct neck. The scales are smooth and highly polished and in general appearance it may at first glance resemble a Black Cobra, but the pale underparts and rich yellow throat are quite distinctive, as is the well-fitting skin around the neck. (In the cobras the skin looks loose in the neck region when the hood is not spread.) It is a snake with a distinctive "look" about it, made up of a combination of scale pattern and texture, shape of body and general attitude, and a naturalist soon learns to recognise it at a glance.

Although Smyth's Water Snake can live out of water, it finds all or most of its food there, the long sloping teeth being well adapted to catch slippery prey like mud-fish and clawed frogs. In captivity it accepts a variety of small fish and frogs, but does well only if given plenty of water space. It has the reputation of striking freely when first caught and one should perhaps handle it a little cautiously, but I had many pass through my hands and found them docile enough. This is another snake that is generally caught by chance, especially in fish traps of the basket type. It is also worth visiting small streams and pools in the dry season when the women are dividing them into sections and emptying them to catch the fish, and all sorts of strange creatures, including snakes, come to light.

8. The Brown Water Snake (Plate IV)

Natrix anoscopus

The Brown Water Snake is much smaller and less conspicuous, being dull reddish-brown or olive-brown, generally with dark transverse bands, and it seldom reaches two feet in length. Its scales are keeled, and they give the skin a rough, dull appearance. This is the snake of muddy pools of the forest country and it is even more likely to be found than Smyth's Water Snake during fish-catching operations. It was once called *Natrix ferox* and is known in some zoos as the Fierce Snake, though without any very obvious reason. It lives on tiny fish, frogs and tadpoles, and is closely related to the very well known English Grass Snake.

Although some black snakes, both big and small, are extremely poisonous, a number of black or grey snakes are quite harmless. The very small ones are not easy to name, but three groups are distinct enough to be recognised at sight.

9. The West African House Snake (Plate V)

Boaedon lineatus and *virgatus*

The West African House Snake does indeed live up to its name, coming into stores, houses and other buildings in search of the rats and mice on which it feeds, so it is a snake to be encouraged. Although its scales are smooth, they are dull and satiny in appearance and they are in numerous rows, from 23-35 in the various members of this group. The body of the commonest form is blackish (not jet black) or brown; two pale-yellow or white stripes run from the tip of the nose along each side of the face, one over and one under the eye, and reach as far as the back of the head. This is the usual pattern of the forest form of the West African House Snake (*B. virgatus*), but a more closely related kind found mostly in the more open country (*B. lineatus*) has only one such line on either side, passing or going through each eye. The West African House Snake is docile and harmless.

10. The File Snake (Plate V)
Mehelya poensis

It is perhaps misleading to describe the File Snakes as black; dark grey or blackish would be more accurate, while one of them is sometimes brown. They are always uniform in colour above, but the midline of the under-surface, as in many snakes, is often lighter in colour, in this case generally yellowish or cream. This plain colouring, with the distinctive shape, makes the File Snake easily recognisable and the name is a good one, for it does indeed look like a long triangular file, with a clearly marked ridge along the back and almost flat sloping sides; the keeled scales increase the similarity, and they are sometimes rather separated, showing the paler skin between them. The head is flat and the unusually blunt nose is almost straight across (see Plate VI).

File Snakes take only cold-blooded prey—other snakes, lizards and frogs—but snakes frequently seem to be their main diet. In captivity it is fatal to put File Snakes with any others less than about twice their own size, and it was early in my collecting days, while I was still training staff, that I learnt this lesson dearly. In my absence on trek a large File Snake was brought in, recognised as harmless, and put in with a mixed harmless collection. It fed very well indeed and two of its victims were rare snakes that I never saw or took again! When a victim longer than itself is eaten, the tail hangs out until the head end is digested.

File Snakes are found in both forest and grassland and are often described as tree snakes, but my specimens were mostly taken in clearings, either on the ground or on concrete structures, perhaps only because they were more easily seen and caught there. Four different species of File Snake are recorded for West Africa, differing in details and in distribution but all clearly belonging to this genus. The largest may reach a length of slightly over 4 ft. with the thickness of a man's thumb. All accounts agree that the File Snakes are most inoffensive.

11, 12. The Black Tree Snake *(Plate VI)*
Thrasops occidentalis and *flavigularis*

Only one harmless black snake frequently grows to over 4 ft. and this may even reach just over 7 ft. It is better known as the Black Tree Snake and there are two forms, one in the forest and one in the savannah woodland. These tree snakes are uniformly black or very dark grey, except for the head and throat which are pale grey or yellow, and the under-surface, which is usually a shade paler than the sides and may sometimes have a yellow tinge. The Black Tree Snake is long and slender, and really long specimens are no more than 1 in. thick. The scales are dull and slightly keeled and they are arranged in an easily recognisable pattern, very uniform in shape and in regular vertical layers rather like stacks of bricks. In most parts of the West African forest the Black Tree Snake seems rather rare and the specimens that I caught in 1945 were the first to be recorded for Ghana, but the savannah forest species had been taken earlier in many parts of West Africa.

The Black Tree Snake has an unusually large eye. When frightened or annoyed it inflates the front third of its body by filling the lungs and various air sacs with which snakes are plentifully supplied; when fully inflated it is two or three times its normal thickness, but even when inflated and annoyed, the Black Tree Snake does not attempt to open its mouth or strike. Many snakes inflate themselves to some degree, but no other West African kind behaves just like this, certainly no other black snake. (The hood-spreading of the cobra is a different action, the ribs in the neck region being raised fanwise on each side.)

A very young Black Tree Snake (Pl. VI, 12), the only one that my team ever collected, caused a lot of excitement, for they thought it was a new kind of snake and therefore something to rejoice about. After much searching in my books I realised that the juvenile form of this snake, in both East and West Africa, was quite unlike the adult, having a pretty marbled pattern in black, green and yellow that is lost when the snake assumes its adult colours on reaching a length of perhaps 3 ft.

The species found in the trees of the open country has the Latin name *Thrasops flavigularis*, meaning "yellow-throated", and it generally has this feature even though its body colour may vary. This snake is remarkably like the Boomslang (see Chap. V), a back-fanged snake of the same region, and they have frequently been confused.

Black Tree Snakes take birds, small mammals and lizards, but birds seem to be their main prey.

13. The Egg-eating Snake *(Plate VI)*
Dasypeltis scabra

The Egg-eating Snake, found in many parts of Africa, is one of the most fascinating of all snakes, for it is perfectly adapted to a strange way of living. A number of snakes eat eggs, swallowing them whole and letting them go down into the stomach, where the shell is digested by the stomach juices or perhaps broken by accident, but most of these snakes also take other types of food. The Egg-eating Snake, however, lives on nothing but eggs and one result is that its teeth have almost disappeared. The mouth can open to an astonishing degree to engulf an egg several times its own diameter. As soon as the egg reaches the gullet it meets several short bony projections from the backbone, tipped with enamel, which at once break it. The contents are swallowed and the crushed shell is spat out.

This is another snake with a "look" about it which can be easily remembered but is much less easy to describe, because colour is almost meaningless; even in the same general area it may be dirty white, rufous, olive or various shades of brown or black, with or without several different patterns of spots, bands or blotches. Its largely nocturnal and arboreal habits make it difficult to find and it was always a welcome arrival at my house. I took only about six specimens, all of the same colour variety—a pale brown with scattered and rather irregular darker markings and a series of very narrow bright yellow, almost gold, rings.

The Egg-eating Snake seldom reaches 3 ft. in length. There is no distinct neck and the body is more or less the same thickness throughout. The eye, with its vertically narrow pupil, is distinctive: the scales are so rough that they rub against each other with a hissing sound. It is found in both forest and savannah country, on the ground and in trees, especially in the neighbourhood of weaver-birds' nests. In areas with marked dry and rainy seasons and, therefore, fairly clear-cut breeding periods, the Egg-eater has a hard time in the off-season and presumably lives on the fat store laid down when eggs are plentiful, but it is not quite confined to birds' eggs. I have known one eat its own eggs and I have little doubt that it will also take the hard-shelled eggs of various small lizards as well as the pea-sized eggs of the giant snail.

THE AFRICAN GREEN SNAKES

We now come to the most difficult group of all—the harmless green snakes. About twelve kinds of active snakes are wholly or largely green, with heads and bodies covered with fairly large scales or shields. (In addition there are three tree vipers, of sluggish habit, whose heads are covered with numerous tiny rough scales.) Of these 12 active snakes, 9 are harmless, 2 are mambas (forest) and 1 is the poisonous back-fanged snake, the Boomslang (savannah woodlands). Only these three and one of the harmless snakes which is so rare as to be best overlooked (with only one specimen recorded for Ghana up to 1958) normally exceed 4 ft., and it therefore seems safe to say that all green snakes over 5 ft. long are poisonous, wherever they may be found.

For a long time one group of African green snakes had the name *Chlorophis* (literally, green snakes), but zoologists now call them all *Philothamnus* (thicket-lovers). This genus has five species in both forest and savannah woodland in West Africa but they are not easy to distinguish, even in the hand. They may be bright green, with or without some darker markings, but they vary in colour between pale vivid green and black, so that the only certain way of naming them is by scale-counts. One distinctive feature is that the scales are smooth and shiny, while in most other green snakes they are either rough, as in the Emerald and Green-lined Snakes, or dull, as in the mambas. The African Green Snakes, as they can best be called, reach about 4 ft. in length, but the average one seen is considerably below that. They spend most of their time in trees and bushes; some of them specialise in living on the reeds around water, but all are very much at home in the water, swimming strongly with the head held well above the surface. The chief diet of these African Green Snakes is probably frogs, but they also take lizards and even fish, while they have been known to catch weaver birds.

Plate V

14. Green-lined Snake
15. Emerald Snake
9. West African House Snake
10. File Snake

Plate VI

13.

12.

11.

13. Egg-eating Snake

12. Black Tree Snake—Juvenile
11. Black Tree Snake—Adult

Plate VII

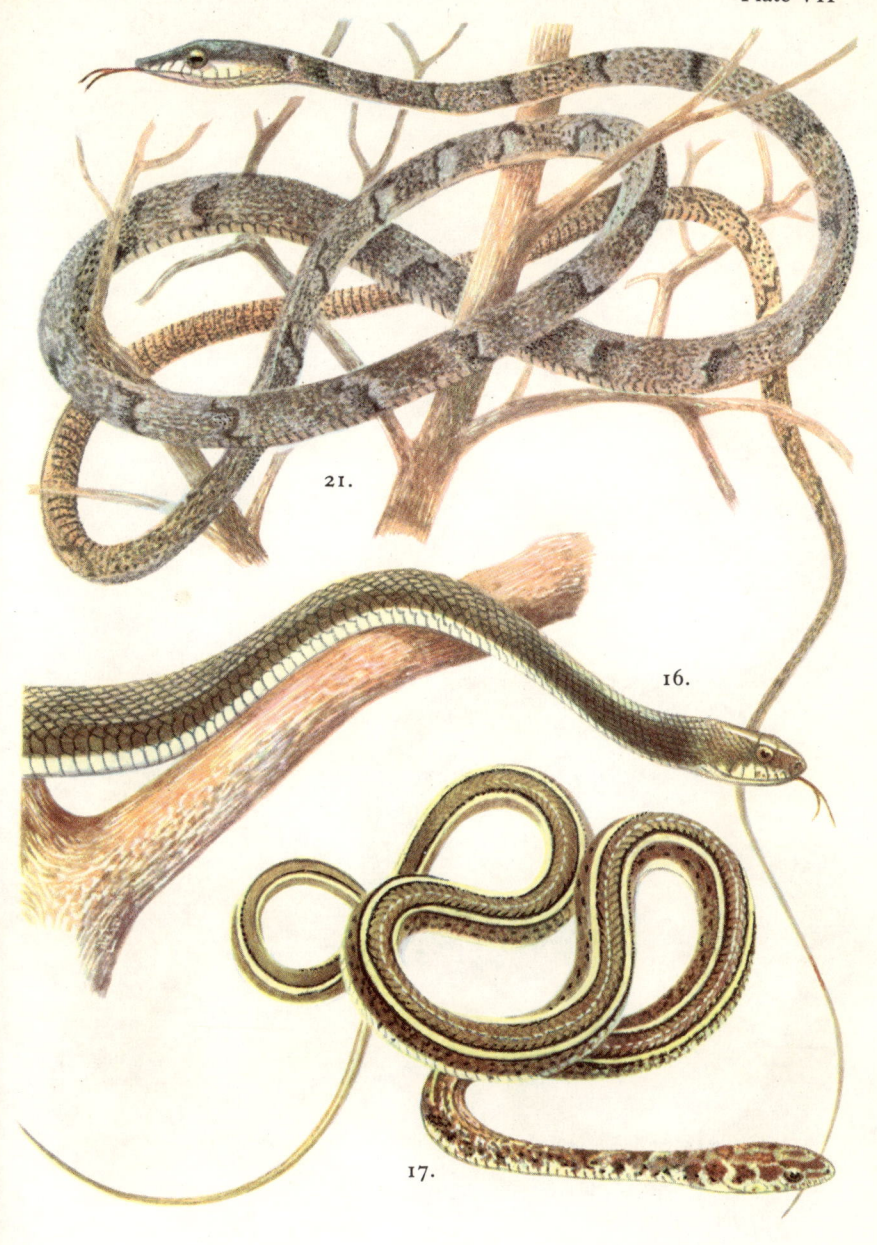

21. Twig or Vine Snake
16. African Beauty Snake—Plain Form
17. African Beauty Snake—Striped Form

Plate VIII

20. The Burrowing Snake   18. Rufous Beaked Snake

14. The Green-lined Snake (*Plate V*)
Hapsidophrys lineata

15. The Emerald Snake (*Plate V*)
Gastropyxis smaragdina

Two of the commonest snakes in the forest clearings can best be known as the Green-lined Snake and the Emerald Snake. Unlike the African Green Snakes they have keeled scales which give the skin a rough texture. In the Green-lined Snake the scales are black, with green keels, giving a distinctive black-and-green-lined appearance, while in the Emerald Snake the whole of each scale is green, but this one has a distinct dark eye stripe. Both reach a length of about 4 ft. and both have long tails; in the Emerald Snake the tail is always just over one-third of the total length, and in the other always just under one-third, but these long-tailed snakes easily lose a bit of tail and one should check carefully that the tail is complete. Little seems to have been recorded about their feeding habits, but I found both lizards and frogs in their stomachs.

A fairly large brown snake, which could be known as the White-spotted Beaked Snake, leads an underground life in sandy country. The head is scarcely distinct from the body and the snout ends in a very distinct beak, forming an efficient burrowing tool. It is pale brown, with or without black and white spots, and though it reaches a length of more than 5 ft. it seems to feed mainly on insects. It is similar to the Rufous Beaked Snake which belongs to the back-fanged section of the family.

One small snake, *Neusterophis variegatus*, apparently with no common native or English name, might well be called the Cocoa Farm Snake, for it is often seen on or among dead cocoa leaves. It is seldom as long as 12 in. and although it opens its mouth in a threatening way it is not at all poisonous. Its general colour is red and brown, with faint black and white specks on the side and a white mark around the neck. It feeds on small frogs.

The White-spotted Snake has a tiny white spot on each of its blue-black scales and the second part of its scientific name, *Prosymna meleagris*, refers to this feature, for it means "guinea fowl". This harmless snake is under 1 ft. long and lives in the dry country north and south of the forest. It is a burrower and probably feeds on insects.

CHAPTER V

BACK-FANGED SNAKES

This first group of poisonous snakes forms a sub-family of the huge family of *Colubrid* snakes and they are known generally as back-fanged or slightly poisonous snakes. With one exception, they are snakes that are not dangerous to human beings. Both upper and lower jaws have solid teeth and in addition there are deeply grooved, but not fully hollow, teeth at the rear of the teeth on the upper jaw (maxillary) and more or less below the eye. They are so placed that the snake can hardly "strike" with them and the poison can only be injected when the victim is gripped firmly in the jaws. Some 30 members of the group, belonging to 16 genera, are recorded in West Africa and there is no quick or easy way of distinguishing them as a group from the harmless kinds, though some of them are distinct enough and easily recognisable. Examination of the mouth is the only exact way of identifying them, but with small specimens this is not at all easy.

The strange thing about this group is that some of them have very similar "opposite numbers" in the non-poisonous part of this family. For instance, the Black Tree Snake is surprisingly like the Boomslang even in scale details, and the White-spotted Beaked Snake (harmless) is very like the Rufous Beaked Snake (back-fanged). At the same time one of the black burrowing back-fanged snakes, *Calamelaps*, has such an astonishing resemblance, scale by scale, with the very venomous Burrowing Vipers that experts have been confused.

Seven of the 16 genera found in West Africa are either rare or subterranean, and most of these are small, less than 2 ft. in length; a few do not even reach 1 ft. A notable point about the back-fanged group is that brown and black are the two main colours, while a number are very noticeably striped. Green is rare and only two species are recorded as being wholly or largely green. In the Boomslang, to be described shortly, green is but one of its colour forms.*

The back-fanged snakes as a whole, and not only the more conspicuous and easily recognisable kinds dealt with here, are more common in the open grass country of West Africa than in the high forest, and this may be why so few are coloured green.

THE SAND SNAKES

People living in the open country of West Africa, whether along the coast or to the north of the tropical forest, are used to

* The rare *Dipsadoboa*, with no popular name, also has several colour varieties and its green form is best described as dull olive, with yellow underparts. This is an inhabitant of the forest and grows to a length of about 3 ft., but has seldom been collected; the three specimens which I took in the old Central Province around Oda were the first, and possibly the only, ones recorded for Ghana.

seeing a number of conspicuously striped snakes, mostly rather thin for their length, and all tending to be active snakes. There are six species of these striped snakes and they belong to three different genera. One is rare (*Rhamphiophis togoensis*), but the others are common enough and they are among the most variable snakes in the area, differing in both colour and pattern even around the same town.

Unfortunately it is extremely difficult to describe these striped snakes in a way that will allow the ordinary observer to distinguish them. *Psammophis*, meaning sand snake, is widespread in Africa and extends east far into Asia. Three species are known in West Africa, of which one, *P. chokari*, is found only in the very dry zones. It reaches 5 ft. and may be brown, yellow or grey, with two rather variable but darker lateral lines and one vertebral line.

The two other species of *Psammophis* have the names of *elegans* and *sibilans*; the latter means "hissing", but this does not seem a very appropriate name for a snake which does not hiss in the terrifying manner of the big vipers. *P. elegans*, known as the Striped Beauty Snake, is slender, perhaps the most slender of these striped snakes, and one of the most markedly striped.

16. The African Beauty Snake (Plain form)   (*Plate VII*)
Psammophis sibilans

17. The African Beauty Snake (Striped form) (*Plate VII*)
Psammophis sibilans

P. sibilans is of heavier build, smooth and rather sleek, with a body thickness of about 1 in. in 4 ft. specimens in good condition. This is plentiful in many parts of the open country, but has so many different phases that it is best described as follows: colour very variable; brown, more or less mixed with olive above, with or without brown or yellow lines, sometimes but not always bordered with black, and these lines are sometimes broken; cream or yellow beneath. This kind may reach between 5 and 6 ft. in length, but the average one seen crossing the road, or basking in the sun while resting gracefully on low shrubs, is not more than 4 ft. long.

P. sibilans is sometimes known as the African Beauty Snake; with its pretty striping and often rather noticeable head pattern, the name is a good one. It has invaded the forest clearings in some parts of West Africa and there developed into a new colour form in which the stripes have disappeared; the upper side is uniformly olive brown, with the scales narrowly margined with black. The underparts are uniformly yellowish and in young specimens the throat is often red. This could well become known as the Olive Grass Snake. Like its striped forms, it takes small rodents, birds, lizards and frogs; it is an active snake and pursues the slower prey determinedly through the grass.

Two members of the genus *Dromophis* are found in the grasslands. Both are normally striped, one with three pale and the other with three dark lines, but they are much smaller snakes than the African Beauty Snake and its relatives, and they reach a length of only 3 ft. 6 in. and 2 ft. respectively.

18. The Rufous Beaked Snake *(Plate VIII)*
Rhamphiophis oxyrhynchus

This is a snake of the drier sandy country. It is another handsome snake, pale brown above, the scales having darker points which sometimes give the effect of a series of very narrow stripes along the body. The name is suitable, for the nose is prolonged forward and down in the form of a hollow beak, which is presumably used for pushing into the loose sand where it lives. It is an inoffensive snake, seldom biting when touched or handled, but often inflating the throat in display. It takes a wide range of small prey, but in captivity will do well on frogs and small skinks and other lizards.

The Cat Snake (*Tarbophis variegatus*) is a snake of the dry grass woodlands from Guinea to the Cameroons. The usual colour is silvery grey, with irregular black markings above and uniform beneath. The head is very large in proportion and quite distinct from the body. I took several specimens around Accra, all under 20 in., and they fed freely on lizards. The size given by Villiers is about 32 in., but one that I took in Northern Ashanti was slightly larger than that. It has the reputation of being aggressive, but its poison teeth are far back and it cannot bite a human.

19. The Boomslang (*Plate IX*)
Dispholidus typus

Mention has already been made of the Boomslang, the only member of this group said to be capable of giving a serious bite; about seven fatal cases have been reported from South Africa, where the snake is well-known and common and where it received its name of Boomslang (tree snake). It cannot strike, like a front-fanged snake, but can inject its poison only when it has obtained a full grip. This also is a snake of the open country, but living in shrubs and trees, where it may be seen sunning itself in the early morning or evening. It comes to the ground to lay eggs and catch at least part of its food, and it swims freely.

The Boomslang feeds largely on lizards, including chameleons, but it also takes birds and their eggs, and frogs. It is a fairly large snake, reaching a length of nearly 6 ft. It is also one of the most variable in colour. In South Africa it is suggested that males are usually green or black and females red or brown, but it is most unusual for snakes to have such sex differences and this has not been reported from West Africa, where the colours may be black, brown, olive or green with the scales more or less bordered with black. The green form may sometimes be confused with the Green Mamba and, as already mentioned, the black form is astonishingly like the Black Tree Snake, which has the same pattern of regular scales in neat vertical rows. It is thought that all Boomslangs up to a length of about 24 in. are a general brownish colour above and rather mottled or spotted along the sides.

The Boomslang also displays by inflating, but only the throat region is expanded and not the front third of the body. The eye is particularly large. Although it may be aggressive and wild when first caught, it soon settles down in captivity.

20. The Burrowing Snake (*Plate VIII*)
Calamelaps unicolor

Several small back-fanged snakes are burrowing by habit; some live in the forest but most in the open savannah country. They are usually found while digging and most can be identified only by detailed scale counts. One of these burrowing snakes, *Calamelaps unicolor*, is found from Guinea through to East Africa and it is almost identical with the black Burrowing Vipers in both general appearance and in scale details, but it is quite inoffensive and harmless. It reaches a length of about 30 in.

Finally there are two snakes of this group living in the forest, in particular around the forest clearings, which can both be readily recognised.

21. The Twig Snake (*Plate VII*)

Thelotornis kirtlandii

The Twig Snake, *Thelotornis kirtlandii*, is found in many parts of Africa—East, Central and South as well as West—and in some areas it has spread into the savannah zone, but in West Africa it is largely a snake of the forest edge and clearings. Fully grown it is about 5 ft. long, but its body is seldom more than ⅜ in. thick and for its length it is probably the thinnest snake in Africa. The tail is very long—over one-third of the total length. The head is large, long and lozenge-shaped. The general body colour is a fine mixture of greens, greys, browns and pink, the general effect being of a twig covered with lichens, and it is a very effective example of protective coloration. The head is clear green above and whitish or cream below, with a sharp line of division passing through the eye. The pupil of the eye is elliptical, but only in this snake is it horizontal and not vertical.

At the first approach of a possible enemy the Twig Snake keeps still, draped in a gently curved position, often more or less along a branch; if further threatened it inflates two or three inches behind the head to a surprising degree, the skin being stretched until the lines of scales are widely separated and black patches of skin appear.

This snake has a remarkably coloured tongue—vivid red with black tip—which it protrudes and flickers conspicuously to interest and attract lizards or birds which it can then seize. The Twig Snake normally feeds on lizards and other snakes, though it is known also to take birds. In captivity some specimens take small fish freely and in the United Kingdom Zoos this makes it easier to keep them throughout the winter months when lizards are hard to obtain.

Plate IX

22. Blanding's Tree Snake—Black and Brown Varieties   19. Boomslang

Plate X

23. Green Mamba

27. Hoodless Cobra

BACK-FANGED SNAKES

22. Blanding's Tree Snake (*Plate IX*)
Boiga blandingii

Blanding's Tree Snake is the only forest snake, other than the cobras and pythons, that grows to well over 6 ft. in length. There are two colour forms, brown and black, and in shape and pattern they are identical; the head is relatively enormous, and broader in proportion than any other tree snake, while the body is compressed vertically. The smooth scales are so dull and unpolished as to appear almost dusty, in contrast to the shining Black-and-White Cobra, which has a round, compact body. Both black and brown forms have the same markings—large irregular dark diamonds scattered along the whole length; in the pale brown form these marks are a darker brown; in the black form they are merely a denser black and not always very obvious. This form has a distinct black and yellow or cream pattern on the face; the throat is yellow and the belly scales have patches of yellow on them which get less and less until at the base of the tail the scales are wholly grey. The brown form is brown beneath, but its face has the same pattern as in the dark form.

Most of my black specimens were taken around houses and clearings and most of my brown in the farms and forest, but this was probably accidental, and it seems that both forms are found equally everywhere. Both colour forms are distinct at all ages and do not begin the same, as in the Boomslang. The young of the black form is not very different from the adult, but the young brown form is pink with irregular chocolate markings that break up its outline very effectively and make it difficult to pick out in a tree or shrub.

When first caught this snake pretends to be aggressive, opening its mouth and displaying wildly, but I have never known one to strike or do any damage. It preys mainly on birds, such as bulbuls and weavers, and one sometimes takes up its station in a palm or other tree housing a weaver bird colony.

They have been known to take chameleons and in Ghana they are said to eat eggs; they are, in fact, known by the same tree name as the Egg-eating Snake and they eat eggs in captivity. A closely related, but less common, species called *B. pulverulenta*, found in roughly the same area, could be called the Powdery Tree Snake; it grows to only half the other's length and seems to have only one colour form, best described as dirty pink with irregular pale brown diamonds. In the hand, the larger kind is found to have some 21 to 25 rows of scales and the smaller only 19.

CHAPTER VI

COBRAS AND MAMBAS

The cobras and mambas belong to another family with a wide distribution. Most of the well known poisonous snakes in Africa and Asia belong to it; there are several deadly representatives in America, and even more in Australia. Only Europe is without any.

A detailed description of a snake's fangs and the various types of venom and their effect is given in Chapter VIII. It is enough to mention here that these Elapine snakes have front fangs always erect in position. Their venom is rather small in volume but very potent, and it acts quickly on parts of the nervous system. There is much misunderstanding about the mambas and it cannot be stressed too often that the so-called Black Mamba does not reach West Africa. It is a South and East African snake, reaching as far north as Angola on the west and Kenya and Uganda in the east and centre. What is more, this notorious mamba is never a true black, like the commonest colour phase of some of the cobras, but at its darkest a dusky brown or bronze.

23. The Green Mambas *(Plate X)*
Dendroaspis viridis and *jamesonii*

West African mambas are all green and there are two species. Hallowell's Green Mamba seems confined to West Africa, while Traill's Green Mamba is a typically Central and East African species, reaching across to Eastern Nigeria and the Cameroons, where it appears to be the more common kind. Its range just extends into Ghana, where I took one specimen in riverain forest a few miles outside Accra during the recent war. It is similar to the common species in colour, general appearance and habits, and distinguished from it mostly by its different scale count; Traill's Green Mamba has 15 to 19 rows of scales in the middle of the body, while Hallowell's Green Mamba, the species so common in Ghana, has only 13 rows. At close range this difference might be obvious, but it is simplest here to group them and speak simply of the Green Mamba.

The Green Mamba is yet another snake which is almost unmistakable, whatever its length. Its green scales have a matt, almost velvety, surface, and the lateral scales are shorter than those along the back and set obliquely. Most scales have a dark or even black margin and these are particularly noticeable around the lips; the dark edging to the scales of the tail is also obvious and the general effect is that the tail seems to be plaited. Above all, the Green Mamba has an alive, active look about it, balancing itself perfectly among the branches and with the front part of the body held free on the alert. There is a fairly distinct neck, in contrast to the cobras, where there is practically no narrowing behind the head. Two colour forms of Hallowell's Green Mamba are found in Ghana; one is a pure green, best described as bottle green, while the other has a distinct tinge of brown or orange in it, especially towards the tail. The two colour forms are found side by side and seem equally numerous. No other colour forms seem to occur, and, according to most accounts, Traill's Green Mamba is similar in colour though the tail is sometimes described as blackish.

Although Green Mambas spend much time in trees they are quite at home on the ground and can swim strongly. They are more active than the average snake, but cannot exceed about 6 m.p.h. In a large shrub or tree they quickly put themselves out of reach and can seldom be caught without cutting down the tree.

In West Africa Traill's Green Mamba is known to reach a length of 8 ft. and Hallowell's Green Mamba rather over 7 ft., but in parts of East Africa the former grows much longer. In the West African forest many are caught measuring between 5 and 6 ft. in length, but anything over 7 ft. is sufficiently unusual to be noteworthy. The longest which I measured personally measured exactly 7 ft., but at least one live specimen sent to the London Zoo was rather longer. At all lengths, but especially from 4 ft. upwards, the Green Mamba is much less bulky than the Black-and-White and the Black-necked Cobras.

In other parts of Africa mambas defend their breeding territory and this is likely to be true in West Africa also, but I have not come across any reports of it or experienced it personally. The aggressive habits of snakes about which so much is said probably have to do with such defence of breeding grounds during the breeding season. I have heard of only one report of a Green Mamba showing aggression: this snake came

COBRAS AND MAMBAS

through the crown of a tree and made some threatening movements, but did not press home its attack.

Captive Green Mambas must be treated with even more caution than cobras. They usually remain alert and prepared at any time to strike with little or no provocation, and they are ever ready to slip out if the chance offers. They often feed greedily, striking at any animal put into their cage; a mouse is killed in about 30 seconds. The mamba's normal food is warm-blooded prey, and birds and small mammals are accepted equally in captivity. Perhaps they tend to take small rather than large animals, for in the many that we caught alive there were seldom any obvious bulges. On one occasion a large Hallowell's Green Mamba killed and swallowed its cage mate of the same species and practically the same size, but it died a week or so after this meal. Such behaviour in captivity does not mean that it is usual in the wild.

Mamba bites can certainly be fatal to humans. There may be little sign of damage at the actual site of the bite so that deaths from mamba bite can easily go undetected, especially if received on the head or body, which is more likely with such an active tree snake. There is little doubt that people are killed by Green Mambas in every part of West Africa every year, and I therefore find it rather strange that in my 14 years in the Ghana forest, constantly enquiring about snakes and, for the latter part of my service, collecting very many of them, the only mamba bites of which I had experience happened to men handling a mamba carelessly or trying to catch one. Two bites on the hand were treated immediately by the "cut and suck" method; one case, the more serious one, also received antivenin within some 15 minutes of the bite being inflicted. The third case was a boy bitten on the lower leg while he was foolishly trying to catch a mamba in his hat! He was not treated until 2 or 3 hours after the incident, but he recovered, as did the other two.

Although the Green Mambas in West Africa are typically snakes of the high forest and riverain forest they are now most frequently seen in and around clearings and the majority of those which we caught were taken in farms and secondary forest.

Some authorities describe a slight puffing of the throat in mambas when they are alarmed or about to strike, but I did not observe this in Hallowell's Green Mamba. A more typical movement is the rather unusual tongue action; in most snakes the tongue is normally moved out and in, with perhaps a quivering of the forked end, but the mamba often protrudes its tongue fully and then moves it up and down slowly, bending it at the point where it leaves the lips. Little has been recorded about the breeding habits of Green Mambas; they are, of course, egg-layers, like the great majority of their family, but no information is available as to their breeding seasons in West Africa or size of average clutch.

THE COBRAS

Three typical cobras are found within our area; the Black-necked or Spitting Cobra of the open country and some of the larger coastal clearings; the Black Cobra of the high forest zone; and the Egyptian Cobra, which is found in sub-desert regions. This latter is local and scarce within our region, but because of their size, colour and active habits the other two are probably the two most familiar West African poisonous snakes.

24. The Black-necked or Spitting Cobra   (*Plate XI*)
Naja nigricollis

The name Spitting Cobra needs explanation. This snake lives mostly in open grass woodlands where it is in danger of being trampled on by cattle, antelopes, etc. To protect itself it can spray a fine jet of poison at the face and eyes of the intruder and it can do this because the opening of the poison fang is in the

COBRAS AND MAMBAS

front and not at the tip. This venom can travel several feet and is directed accurately; if some touches the eyes it causes intense pain and inflammation, and it may result in permanent weakness. Any dilute watery fluid should be used to wash out the eyes as quickly as possible and the sooner this is done, the less damage results. This "spitting" is a defence against intruders; to kill its prey this cobra uses its fangs normally. It takes a wide variety of food, including insects, other snakes and eggs, but there is no mention of fish among its usual diet.

This cobra is extremely variable in colour, but in all parts of its range in West Africa the commonest form is a dark slate grey, almost black on the sides and upper surface, and with a completely black band, 7 or 8 scales wide, across the throat, from which the name Black-necked (*nigricollis*) is derived. There is usually a patch of red or salmon pink scales below the neck which is clearly seen when the cobra rears up to display or spit. All colour forms have a distinctly dull appearance; the scales are never polished or shiny, as in the Black Cobra of the high forest. Two other colour varieties frequently described, especially in other parts of its range, are brown or olive, with dark-edged scales, and yellowish beneath, and uniform brown, with yellowish beneath. My team collected two remarkable Spitting Cobras in the Northern Territories of Ghana, best described as uniform coppery red. One was 5 ft. long and in perfect condition when sent to the London Zoo; the other was smaller, just 26 in. long, and it was identified by Loveridge as *var. pallida*, a form known from the desert areas of Central Africa.

This is the smallest of the three West African cobras and the average snake caught or seen is distinctly shorter than in the Black Cobra, nor does it seem to reach the very heavy size sometimes found in the latter. The maximum recorded for West Africa appears to be 7 ft. 4 in., but anything above 6 ft. is big. Although it is a strong, active snake, an experienced person can safely catch one, provided that he wears adequate goggles to protect the eyes. Venom drops cannot hurt unbroken skin, though this should be washed off as quickly as possible.

When the cobra's hood is spread its identity is clear enough, but this is done only in fear or anger; at rest or on the move the hood lies collapsed along the sides of the neck and is visible only as rather loose skin; this is true of all the "hooded" cobras. In the neck region the ribs are much longer than those lower down and there are also more rows of scales, so that for identification purposes one must be careful to take counts near the centre of the body.

The Black-necked Cobra's original range was in the open savannah country around and north of the high forest zone, but it has also spread into many of the coastal strips from which the forest has now disappeared. Thus it is now common around Freetown, Takoradi and Sekondi; in such areas it may be expected to occur alongside the Black Cobra and this is also true of the rather mixed zone along the actual edge of the forest where their ranges meet, but in most of West Africa it is more usual to find either the one *or* the other.

Like all cobras, the Black-necked Cobra lays eggs; little has been recorded about its breeding, but one presumes that egg-laying normally takes place in the early rainy season, to provide moist hatching conditions and to allow the young to emerge while plenty of insects, young rodents, etc., are available for food. The newly hatched young measures about 18 in. long.

25. The Black Cobra *(Plate XI)*
Naja melanoleuca

The Black Cobra, sometimes called Black-and-White Cobra, of the West and Central African forests, also varies in colour but in West Africa most are either black or very dark slate grey above and on the sides, with the under-surface a shade lighter and with clearly defined cream markings on the lips. It may also be brown with black markings, or entirely banded along the whole length of the body; there is also a wide variation in the colour and pattern of the under-surface. It seems safe to say, however, that it never has either the black band or the red patch of the Black-necked Cobra on the throat and neck. In a wild snake the hood is spread without much provocation, especially if the snake is cornered; sometimes the hood has a clear white pattern above, but this is often irregular and it is seldom, or perhaps never, in the form of spectacles so familiar in the Indian Cobra.

Whatever the colour, it always has brightly polished scales, and this character is very easily recognised, even at some distance. The Black Cobra is alert and active, equally at home on the ground, in trees or in water, and when at rest it often moves its head restlessly from side to side; it does this at first in captivity, but usually settles down quickly and often becomes reluctant to strike, even when deliberately roused. The juvenile cobra frequently has a series of narrow, irregular white bands, often only a scale or two wide, and these usually persist to a length of about 4 ft. but occasionally to 6 ft.

Many Black Cobras reach a length of 6 or 7 ft.; specimens over 7 ft. are not particularly uncommon, but one of 8 ft. in length is big for anywhere in Africa. Prior to 1946 the longest recorded for West Africa was rather under 8 ft., but within a short period my team caught three live females each measuring just over 8 ft. 8 in. Since then it has been noted that a cobra used by snake-charmers in Sierra Leone measured rather over 9 ft. Of the three very long ones handled by my team, one was of normal girth; the other two were of exceptional size and almost as thick as my wrist.

Anyone experienced in handling snakes should have no difficulty in catching these cobras, but it must be remembered that they can be extremely strong as well as venomous. Although it can climb well enough, this cobra usually tries to escape along the ground or into a hole. The graceful smooth movements of the shining body may give the impression of great speed, but it cannot do more than 6 m.p.h. and a cobra on easy ground is usually overtaken in a few strides by anyone wanting to catch it—or rapidly outdistanced by anyone wishing to run the other way!

Some authorities claim that the Black Cobra is largely nocturnal, spending the day under cover or in a hole; while this may be true in general, it is not unusual to encounter these cobras on the move and active during the daytime.

The Black Cobra eats a wide range of animals—rats and other mammals, lizards, toads, birds and their eggs. In Central Africa some live almost entirely in the lakes, taking only fish. The bite of this cobra can be rapidly fatal, especially to warm-blooded animals; the fangs are rather short, but the venom is concentrated and quick-acting. This cobra is widely but wrongly referred to as the notorious Black Mamba, and people therefore expect it to behave similarly; any threatening movement is thus claimed as aggression. I made wide enquiries on this point and found most claims to be without foundation—the attack had usually come from the person concerned and the cobra was merely defending itself or trying to escape. I heard of only one case in which the snake appeared to open the attack, but the victim died and the full story could not be checked, though he made a statement before he died. He was a Northern Region labourer working in a pineapple farm in the eastern part of Ghana; a Black Cobra attacked and bit him on the leg and when he turned to escape he was pursued and bitten again twice, on the heel and at the back of the leg. This happened in July, which is at the end of the main rainy season, and it is reasonable to assume that the cobra was defending its breeding territory. Aggressiveness in snakes is still a matter of argument and any clear cases of aggression in the cobra, or any other snake, should be reported; the *Nigerian Field* publishes notes, and I am sure that any zoologists on the staff of the various University Colleges and Colleges of Technology in West Africa would be glad to have details for record purposes.

Throughout the forest of Ghana this cobra is well known by the name of oprammiri (the meaning of the first part is not clear, but the second half means black), but this name is applied equally to both species.

Although this is a snake which likes forest cover, it has not deserted the clearings made within the forest and it is very common in farms and on the outskirts of town and village clearings, finding more ample food supplies there than in the closed forest itself. Most of my own specimens came from these clearings; some were spotted by my own men, others were reported by farmers or schoolchildren, while a few were caught in traps or snares and rescued before being seriously damaged. We always did our best to take them alive, but some were brought in dead or died after arrival and these were always examined for parasites, stomach contents, etc. It was rather exceptional to find anything identifiable in the stomach and it seemed strange that in places with so much suitable prey these cobras apparently fed rather infrequently. An animal the size of a Black Rat would be digested fully in from 3–7 days, so the majority of our specimens had not fed for something like a week before death. Like so many tropical animals, these cobras carry many parasites, both external and internal, including Guinea Worm: one large specimen which we took at Oda had no less than eight of these strange worms living in its tissues and forming the typical sores.

26. The Egyptian Cobra *(Plate XII)*
Naja haje

This cobra has a wider distribution than either of the others, being found from Morocco in the north through Egypt and

Eastern Africa down to as far south as Natal, and being most numerous round the edge of the Sahara desert. If found in West Africa at all, it will be along the desert edge and not very far from water courses. The neighbourhood of Lake Chad is a possible locality. Reports vary about its maximum length, but Pitman records one of 8 ft. 6 in. and suggests that it may reach over 9 ft. Most authorities agree that it is more massive than the others and a Sudan specimen of $7\frac{1}{2}$ ft. had a maximum thickness of nearly 3 in. The Egyptian cobra varies in colour but is generally one or more shades of brown for the most part.

27. The Hoodless Cobra *(Plate X)*
Pseudohaje nigra

One other cobra is native to parts of the forest of West Africa. It is rare and rather unlikely to be found, but so little has been recorded about it that it is worth noting my few encounters with it. There are actually two forms of this so-called Hoodless Cobra; one, with the scientific name of *Pseudohaje goldi*, is generally found to the east of our area and the other, *P. nigra*, from Ghana westwards. Towards the end of my tour of service at Oda one of my old hunter friends came in, a man who had been especially successful in getting rare material; this time, he said, he had brought something new, a Black Cobra which looked rather like a Green Mamba. It had no native name of its own but that certainly was an apt description, for it had the shiny scales of a Black Cobra with the slender lines of the mamba and it was both water-loving and tree-climbing. Unfortunately he had had to kill the snake to stop it escaping, but it was fresh and in perfect condition, the first authentic Ghana specimen. Not long afterwards a Forest Guard brought in another from the same area of wet forest; it had been caught in a wire snare set on a game trail and though it was just alive when found, it was dead before he got to me.

COBRAS AND MAMBAS

My next encounter with this rare cobra was a bit of luck. We were returning to station from the usual end of the month pay and reports trip around the district and as we came to a riverside village the people shouted that they had a snake for us. There in an empty cane fish trap was a magnificent Hoodless Cobra! A pile of new funnel-entrance traps stood waiting to be taken down to the river and the snake had just gone into one and coiled up. We quickly undid the end of the trap and dropped the cobra straight into a snake bag that was always kept ready. A few days later it reached London Zoo by air, and, literally, had never been touched by hand. Perhaps it was for this reason that it lived for several years and made a fine exhibit, probably my rarest contribution to the Reptile House there.

I saw this snake only once again: driving back to Kumasi, along a fast new part of the road which ran on a slight embankment through wet forest, I spotted a fine Hoodless Cobra, 6 or 7 ft. long on the side of the road: I braked hard and leapt out of my car, but it just reached the swampy forest before I could grab it.

The two dead specimens measured just under and just over 7 ft., and all four that I saw were uniform in colour. The head and body above are satiny blue-black, the chin white and the throat and the front third of the belly pale yellow; the ventral scales gradually become black-edged and darker, so that the colour changes from yellow to slaty blue at the root of the tail. The eye is very large; the tail is much longer in proportion than in the Black and Spitting Cobras, being almost a quarter of the total length; the head is also broader. It appears to feed mostly on amphibians and the one which I sent to the London Zoo lived for several years entirely on frogs and toads. Nothing seems to be recorded about its venom.

It is perhaps as well to mention also the Water Cobra, a large member of this group which is known to be found in the larger rivers and lakes from the Cameroons in the west through the Congo to as far east as Uganda. It is a water snake, apparently feeding only on fish, and it grows to at least 8 ft.; its general colour is brown, with 20 or more complete black rings along the length of the body, and its scales are shiny. Snakes which spend all or most of their time in the water are hard to observe and collect, and it may well turn out that this large cobra is found in some of the lakes and rivers of Nigeria or even Ghana. It is armed with fangs typical of the cobra family but it seems to have none of the aggressive character found in some of its relatives.

Only one other member of the Elapine family occurs in West Africa, so it may well be mentioned. Best known as the Black Garter Snake, it reaches a length of about 2 ft. and is a snake of the savannah woodlands, living underground or in heaps of soil and rubbish. Its colour is mainly dark grey or black, generally with a number of bands of fine white speckling, though one form is "beautifully banded in coral pink and white", to quote Loveridge. It is generally agreed that this shy, small snake is inoffensive.

CHAPTER VII

VIPERS

Some 15 vipers are found in West Africa, varying in size, habitat, external appearance and behaviour: almost the only thing they have in common is the dentition which shows them to be vipers, that is, they are armed with long, curved poison fangs attached to small bones hinged in the front of the upper jaw in such a way that the teeth can swing up and back, and rest

VIPERS

safely along the roof of the mouth. By this means the fangs can be much longer and finer than in snakes whose fangs are always erect in position. Breakages and loss of fangs do in fact occur, but vipers, like cobras and mambas, normally have several reserve fangs waiting to come forward into position and take over as soon as required. In all species the fangs are fully hollow to the tip and needle-sharp; the volume of venom available is usually large and its main action is on the blood and tissues, though in some species, notably the giant vipers, it also has some effect on the nervous system. (See also Chapter VIII.)

28. The Night Adder *(Plate XIII)*
Causus rhombeatus

The Night Adder is perhaps the best with which to start, for it is the commonest viper in and around towns and villages. It seems likely that it was once an inhabitant of the savannah forest but colonised man-made clearings to feed on the Common Toad, its chief prey, which had already moved in. The Night Adder is now typical of the bare land in and around compounds, where it emerges at dusk to look for food. Though less sluggish than many vipers, it is slow-moving and more likely to be encountered and trodden on unseen than almost any other kind. It is quite usual for small children to wander into the compound after dark, with no more than open sandals on their feet. The natural reaction of a small snake when trodden on is to strike at the intruder, inflicting a bite on the toes, foot or ankle. In my experience the victims did not worry unduly, and even without much treatment suffered no serious damage, but it may be that these were exceptional. There are accounts of two zoo workers, in the United States and United Kingdom, being bitten while handling Night Adders rather carelessly and becoming dangerously ill; perhaps the drastic treatment which they received from enthusiastic colleagues did not help them!

In contrast to most poisonous snakes, in which the poison glands are confined to the area near the base of the fangs, the night adder has large poison sacs extending back through the neck region. The Night Adder's poison does not always seem to be quickly effective against the toad and often one is seen trying to swallow a toad that is still alive and inflated far beyond the stretch of the adder's mouth. It is held like that until the poison finally takes effect.

Slow-moving snakes can either "freeze" to remain unnoticed, or inflate themselves and thus appear much bigger than they are. In some vipers, including the Night Adder, this inflation extends to the whole length of the body, and, like the subsequent deflation, it makes a loud hissing noise.

Most Night Adders are between 12 and 18 in. but they may exceptionally reach about 3 ft. The colour varies considerably but the great majority seen are a shade of khaki, sometimes inclining to reddish, sometimes to olive, with a number of small, irregular, diamond-shaped groups of 4–6 dark scales scattered erratically; there is generally a fairly well-marked dark V on the head and neck. A handsome dark-green form is also found in West Africa but I took only one of this type out of well over a hundred, and this came from near Tamale in the Northern Region of Ghana. Unlike many vipers, the Night Adder has smooth scales, but the scales are dull rather than polished and the head is covered with a few clearly seen plates. In breeding habits it also differs from most vipers, being egg-laying and not viviparous. The eggs may be laid in small batches at intervals of a month or two throughout much of the year, rather than in one or two big batches at more or less definite seasons, and, as in many snakes, one mating can fertilise several batches of eggs.

Plate XI

24. Spitting or Black-Necked Cobra   25. Black Cobra

Plate XII

29. Puff Adder   26. Egyptian Cobra

VIPERS
THE GIANT VIPERS

The members of the genus *Bitis*, a wholly African genus, are known appropriately enough as the giant vipers. The three largest ones are well distributed over the African continent and they are very well known in West Africa. The Puff Adder is found throughout the savannah woodlands and the Gaboon and Rhinoceros Vipers in most of the tropical forest. In general shape they are rather alike—a heavy, flabby body, a narrow neck and a large flat, rather triangular head which houses a pair of massive curved fangs. All the giant vipers produce a large number of living young. They are slow-moving and often placid, capable of tremendous and noisy inflation when alarmed or angry. They are predominantly nocturnal. Each has its own quite different cryptic pattern and coloration that is highly effective in its own habitat, and this will be described for each in turn. The scales are so markedly keeled that the whole skin is very rough to the touch.

29. The Puff Adder (*Plate XII*)
Bitis arietans

The Puff Adder is probably the best known of these three frightening snakes, for it is the most widespread, occurring in all suitable country south of the Sahara. It is everywhere a snake of the open forest and grasslands and its colouring fits it for the sandy, rather bare soil on which it lives for much of the year, for even in the rainy season the ground usually has bare patches between the numerous clumps of tall grass and it is never completely covered like the cleared grass areas around towns and villages. The Puff Adder's skin is a mixture of browns and buffs, with dark and light chevrons down the back which serve to break up the typical snake shape. The flat head is proportionately rather smaller and less markedly triangular than in the Gaboon Viper.

The Puff Adder has a maximum length of about 5 ft., but this is seldom reached in West Africa, though 4 ft. is not unusual. It is stout and heavy for its length and at 5 ft. it weighs between 10 and 15 lb., depending on its condition and on the length of time since feeding. Like the other giant vipers it cannot move fast enough to pursue prey, but must depend on the prey coming within range as it lies efficiently camouflaged. Warm-blooded animals form its usual food and it does not seem to have any very marked preference.

These giant vipers are described as placid and not easily provoked, but this is only true in comparison with more active snakes such as cobras and mambas, and it is not suggested that they can always be approached carelessly or interfered with. Of the three the Gaboon Viper is generally the most placid.

A successful strike by a Puff Adder on any small warm-blooded animal is rapidly fatal, but the massive injection of venom does more than just kill the victim; it also begins to break down the blood and tissues and thus helps digestion. The damage done to a large animal, such as Man, by an untreated bite can be quite appalling, with severe diffuse bleeding into the tissues and body cavities, generally resulting in death, though this may be much delayed. The Puff Adder can be confused with only one other snake—the Carpet Viper; in West Africa this usually reaches a length of only 12–15 in. so confusion might only arise with a Puff Adder a few months old. Above 10 inches the Puff Adder is relatively very much fatter.

30. The Gaboon Viper   (*Plate XIV*)

Bitis gabonica

The Gaboon Viper is familiar enough to farmers and others in the forest country, and an observant person driving a car at night may spot one on the road, but to the ordinary person this enormous and fantastic snake is but a name. It is beyond doubt the biggest (not the longest) poisonous snake in Africa. Detailed records for West Africa are not numerous but the biggest of which I had personal knowledge measured slightly over 5 ft. and weighed 16 lb. before it gave birth to 59 young of approximately finger thickness and some 12 in. long. One killed more recently in Ashanti was 6 ft. long and weighed over 20 lb.; another reported from Sierra Leone measured no less than 6 ft. 8½ in., which is almost certainly a record length.

The Gaboon Viper can be confused with no other snake and although its geometrical pattern is hard to describe in words it can be seen quite clearly in the coloured plate. These colours become dull and faded, but a freshly sloughed snake is a very striking sight; even so the camouflage value of the pattern as it lies motionless in the dimness of the forest floor is amazing. As a results of this effective camouflage there is always a danger of treading on one unawares, and this is probably the cause of most bites, though hunters have described to me how they have sometimes trodden hard on one and provoked nothing more than a frightening hiss!

In captivity the Gaboon Viper accepts Black Rats and no doubt catches these and other smaller rodents in the farmlands, but well grown specimens often catch considerably larger prey. In Ghana I found Giant Rats, Cane Rats, Brush-tailed Porcupines and Royal Antelopes in their stomachs. The Royal Antelope was fully grown, weighing about 5 lb., but such Cane Rats as I found were small ones and I rather doubt if even a large Gaboon Viper could manage a Cane Rat of 12 or 14 lb. Birds are also eaten, especially such ground-feeding birds as francolins and some of the doves.

In a Gaboon Viper 5 ft. long the fangs are almost 2 in. long; gently curved and with an orifice just behind the sharp tip, they are very like hypodermic needles. Gaboon Vipers are powerful snakes capable of a heavy strike which can send these fangs deep into the tissues, making effective first aid very difficult. In addition the venom, though mostly blood-destroying, has a considerable neuro-toxic content.

31. The Rhinoceros Viper *(Plate XIV)*
Bitis nasicornis

The Rhinoceros Viper is so-called because of the warty horns on the tip of the snout, but much that I have written about the Gaboon Viper applies equally to this species. The two snakes are not usually distinguished by forest folk, though they are, in fact, quite unlike in colour. The geometrical patterns of the Rhinoceros Viper are a fantastic combination of brown, yellow, blue, green, red and black, improbable as this may sound, and only a coloured plate can give any idea of its appearance. It always has a clearly marked black arrow head, but the head of the Gaboon Viper is always light in colour.

The head is smaller and the neck thinner in proportion than in the other two giant vipers and the head is the most markedly triangular. It never seems to reach the huge proportions of the Gaboon Viper, so that a Rhinoceros Viper of 4 ft. is exceptionally big. As in the other giant vipers, the tail is very short, amounting to about one tenth of the total length in males and considerably less in females.

The Rhinoceros Viper has a general range within the tropical forest similar to the Gaboon Viper, but it is often called River Jack because of its liking for moist places. We took fewer specimens than of the Gaboon Viper at all of my various stations and I cannot speak definitely about this point, but I could not see any very clear distinction in the habitats of the two kinds. Some 20 live specimens passed through my hands, and I regarded the Rhinoceros Viper as much less placid and reliable than the Gaboon Viper, and a snake to be handled with extreme caution at all times.

VIPERS

The remaining West African members of the viper family are all confined to specialised habitats—in the dense forest, in the dry grasslands and semi-desert, and underground. The ordinary resident or visitor is not likely to see them, but if he does he should have little trouble in recognising them, except that in the case of the Burrowing Vipers he will usually play for safety and assume that several other kinds may also belong to this vicious group until proved otherwise.

32. The Green Tree Viper *(Plate XIII)*
Atheris chloraechis

The Green Tree Vipers of the forest zone should not be confused with any other snake found in this area. The body is of normal proportions but a broad, flat head is joined to it by a narrow neck, and the head is as broad as the stoutest part of the body. The whole head and body are covered, except beneath, with numerous tiny overlapping scales so strongly keeled that the skin is rough. Three species are recorded for West Africa—Werner's Tree Viper and Hallowell's Tree Viper, from Togo to East Africa, and Schlegel's Tree Viper, from Guinea to the Gaboon (*A. chloraechis*).

All are similar in general appearance and habits, though they differ in details of colouring and of habitat, and the following remarks refer principally to Schlegel's Tree Viper, which is common in parts of the forest zone.

I can find few reports about even this species, so that my remarks are based largely on a considerable series I took in Ghana, especially around Oda in 1945–47. The majority were taken alive and sent straight to the London Zoo with the minimum of handling, so my measurements, scale counts, etc., were not at all complete. Adult specimens are uniform pale green, darkening a little on the sides and towards the tail, and with more or less paired golden spots about one inch apart along the upper surface. The underparts are paler green. In younger specimens, under about a foot in length, this coloration is reversed, that is, they are yellowish with green spots. Although Villiers gives its greatest size as 20 in., this figure is often exceeded and I took several between 24 and 28 in. long.

Most specimens are caught on green shrubs and foliage fairly near the ground, but I cannot say if it lives in taller shrubs and trees, for its camouflage is so good that it remains completely hidden if it keeps still, as is its habit. It shows complete adaptation to arboreal life; it balances itself perfectly on the thinnest twig and the tail is prehensile to the very tip.

Many specialised animals are slow to adapt themselves to captivity and this is no exception. I sent some magnificent specimens to the London Zoo, but none settled down and virtually none fed even once. Some observers in East Africa have found that Tree Vipers feed largely on tree frogs, but other reports say that they prefer small mammals, especially rodents. Captive specimens in Ghana have taken small skinks. The Tree Viper's fangs are long, thin and sharp, but it is usually very inoffensive and there seem to be no records of any human bites.

As in typical vipers, the eggs are carried in the body of the mother until they hatch. None of my dead specimens was gravid and the only record I can find is of an East African female with eleven embryos in it when killed.

33. The Carpet Viper *(Plate XV)*

Echis carinatus

The Carpet Viper is of similar size to the Tree Viper, but it is infinitely more dangerous; it is not slow to strike and its venom is extremely powerful and in some parts of its range it is probably the most dangerous of all the poisonous snakes. It is a

VIPERS

ground snake, active mostly at night, and so all the more likely to be encountered unawares. It has a wide range, from West Africa through Egypt and Arabia to India, and it lives in the drier grass woodland and semi-desert, in fact, in similar country to that inhabited by the Sand Boa. In Ghana it reaches as far south as the Accra Plains, though it is rare there: it is found in various parts of northern Ashanti and the Northern Region, but its range in the other countries does not seem to have been recorded.

In other parts, the Carpet Viper may grow to about 34 in., but for a viper it is always slender for its length, at the maximum length being less than 1 in. thick. Its head is fairly obvious, but not so large in proportion as in the Tree Vipers. It is generally pale sandy brown colour, with darker or reddish mottling and wavy, whitish bars, usually bordered with black, along its length, but this pattern is always irregular and not symmetrical as in the Puff Adder. Like the Tree Vipers, it is covered with numerous tiny scales and these scales are so strongly keeled that it is sometimes called the Saw-Scaled Viper. It is easily roused and is one of the very few snakes that can fairly be called aggressive. Its venon acts slowly on humans, and death may occur up to five days after a bite.

The Carpet Viper emerges from hiding in the evening to hunt its prey, which consists mostly of small rodents, though it is also said to eat insects. Like the Horned Viper, it bears living young.

34. The Horned or Sand Viper *(Plate XV)*

Cerastes cornutus

Travellers in the West African forest sometimes speak of encountering the Horned Cerastes, when they mean the Rhinoceros Viper. The Cerastes, or Horned Viper, is in fact a snake of the driest zone of all—the semi-desert and the desert edge—where it lives in rocky or sandy surroundings. It spends the day hidden beneath a layer of sand, with the eyes almost the only part exposed. The name "horned" comes from the scaly horn which is usually present just behind each eye. It resembles the Carpet Viper in general appearance and proportions, but it is paler, to match its sandy background. The head is broader proportionately than in the Carpet Viper and in this respect it resembles more closely the Tree Viper. Once again information is very incomplete, but the only part of the British West Africa where the Horned Viper might be expected to occur is the extreme north of Nigeria.

This desert viper has evolved exactly the same type of movement for traversing loose sand as have the desert rattlesnakes. This is known as "side-winding", in which the snake throws a series of loops sideways and forwards and has only part of its body in contact with the ground at any time, so that it appears to be moving obliquely across the sand. Although the Horned Viper is rightly feared, it seems much less aggressive and lethal than the Carpet Viper.

35. The Burrowing Vipers (*Plate XIII*)
Atractaspis spp.

Last of all we come to the Burrowing Vipers, a tropical and South African genus of highly specialised burrowing snakes, slender in outline, with heads merging directly into the bodies which are of more or less even thickness throughout their length. The very short sharply tapering tail ends in an abrupt point. The eyes are tiny and the sight poor, and unlike other vipers except the Night Adder, they have smooth scales and their heads are covered with large symmetrical shields. Like the Night Adder, also, they are egg-laying. The Burrowing Viper's body is always firm, compact and more or less cylindri-

Plate XIII

32. Green Tree Viper
35. Burrowing Viper
28. Night Adder

Plate XIV

30.

31.

30. Gaboon Viper   31. Rhinoceros Viper

Plate XV

33. Carpet Viper   34. Horned or Sand Viper

cal. It does not seem to inflate the body when annoyed, but the Burrowing Viper never hesitates to bite and its poison is formidable.

Six species of this most unpleasant snake are found in West Africa, of which I took four in Ghana, but they can be distinguished only by counting and comparing scales; they are very alike in general habits as well as in appearance.

Living underground, they are usually found only by chance. Flooding sometimes forces them to the surface, when they show a habit I have never noticed in any other burrowing snake, arching the front few inches of the body and holding the snout pressed to the soil at a sharp angle. This habit has also been recorded in these snakes in East Africa.

Burrowing Vipers are found widely in West Africa, in both forest and grassland. One or other kind occurs almost all over Ghana, from the dry coastal country around Accra, through the forest and up to the far north, though never very plentifully. At least two of these have a wide range, from the Guinea Coast through Central Africa to Uganda and Egypt, and all seem to depend more on the type of soil than on the vegetation growing on it.

Burrowing Vipers are plain snakes—brown, black or grey— but most of my own specimens happened to be all black. Only one, Hallowell's Burrowing Viper, is usually a paler shade of grey with an almost white tail, but this is rare and I took what was for some years the only Ghana specimen. Burrowing Vipers are usually rather small snakes and they seldom exceed 18 in. in length. In July 1947 at Kumasi I caught a specimen of Reinhardt's Burrowing Viper measuring 31 in., which seems to be at least 5 in. longer than previously recorded for any of the species. This was sent alive to the London Zoo, but, like all other live specimens of this very specialised group that I have come across, it refused to feed in captivity, though it lived for 16 months and kept in fine condition.

It is hard to speak about the feeding habits of snakes which are so poorly known, but their diet is known to include skinks, Worm Snakes, small rodents and shrews.

Experienced collectors agree that a Burrowing Viper is liable to bite as soon as touched. The shape of the head and neck, with the extremely long fangs, enables it to bite a hand holding it, however "correct" the hold may be. My first meeting with this snake—a small one—was a very unpleasant experience. I had only just started collecting snakes and among the first half a dozen to arrive was a Burrowing Viper, held safely in a split palm stick by a small schoolboy. To examine it closely I took it behind the head in the orthodox way, only to be bitten immediately near the tip of my forefinger. Although I cut and bled it at once the potent venom killed the flesh around the bite and I lost the finger-top.

As in most vipers, the venom is of the blood- and tissue-destroying type and the damage that I suffered was what I should have expected. It was little comfort to read in the French text-book by Angel—my only source of information then—that another collector had had exactly the same experience some 15 years previously! Since then I have heard of two other similar accidents and it is quite clear that Burrowing Vipers, and any other small black snakes that might possibly turn out to be vipers, should never be handled alive with a naked hand, even by thoroughly experienced men.

Owing to its dark colour and small size, this small snake is probably responsible for many of the snake bites suffered at night after which the snake is not found or killed. We cannot therefore know just how many casualties it causes, but the experiences of collectors who have been bitten make it clear that the venom is very powerful and it is likely that a severe untreated bite would end in death.

CHAPTER VIII

SNAKE BITE—ITS PREVENTION AND TREATMENT

Prevention is better than cure, as an old English proverb runs, and this applies to snake bite even more than to any ordinary disease, for many people are so terrified of snakes that fear complicates the case and makes it more difficult to treat. The ordinary town-dweller of West Africa is unlikely even to see a dangerous snake, far less be bitten by one. What of those who work in the farms and forest? Most bites are received on the foot, the result of treading on or disturbing a snake that has not been noticed, and such bites can be avoided entirely by wearing ordinary leather shoes or, better still, boots.

While working in the forest, when I was frequently travelling on partly cleared survey tracks, I wore short boots and either puttees or canvas gaiters. These gave complete protection as far as the knee, which was as high as any of the big vipers or cobras would be likely to strike without my seeing them, but in many thousands of miles my precautions were never tested! The boots and gaiters also protected me from the rough ground and sharp tree stumps, which added to my comfort and was healthy. A more serious danger is a snake in a tree—perhaps a Green Mamba hanging over a path—but the mamba generally glides off unseen and I regard the chances of such a bite as most remote. In any case a hat would probably be sufficient protection.

A further bit of general advice. Always look carefully before sitting down or taking hold, which may easily protect you also from sitting on or gripping a scorpion; small brown scorpions are plentiful in many parts and their sting, while not fatal, can be very painful.

Although some snakes are easily recognisable, it is often impossible to distinguish harmless from highly dangerous species, so until you are experienced do not handle any snakes with bare hands unless you know they are harmless. Assume that all "dead" snakes are dangerous until identified, and even then keep fingers away from the fangs. Do not be too badly put off by these warnings. Start by examining carefully every dead snake you find and you will gradually come to know them. Then get used to handling live specimens of harmless kinds and finally, when you have both knowledge and confidence, the dangerous ones. Although snakes are not yet a very popular study, there are a few knowledgeable people who can be consulted, particularly in the Colleges and big Schools. A start has been made in founding small Zoos where many of the local snakes, certainly all the important dangerous ones, will be on show; these collections will be a great help in letting people learn which snake is which.

Throughout the world a snake bite is terribly feared, and even the bite of a non-poisonous snake has been known to cause collapse of the patient through shock and the fear of what might happen. Much of this fear is due to ignorance, so let us consider why a snake bites, and what happens when it does.

Except for some of the small insect-eating snakes, and the Egg-eating Snake, all snakes have fairly obvious teeth. In most kinds these teeth are all solid and are used for seizing the prey and helping to swallow it. A number of others also have poison teeth or fangs; these are hollow or deeply grooved teeth through which poison, or venom as it is often called, can be injected into the snake's prey to kill it. That is the true purpose of a snake's poison—to overcome its prey, which is normally much smaller than the snake; in total bulk it seldom approaches the snake itself, even though it may be much thicker.

SNAKE BITE—PREVENTION AND TREATMENT

Why then is a human being or a domestic animal bitten? In most cases it is purely by accident. At night a child goes out of doors without shoes and steps on a Night Adder, which promptly strikes at the intruder. A hunter steps over a log and puts his foot on a Gaboon Viper and is bitten as the snake reacts in surprise and self-defence. Perhaps a cobra finds itself in a small room or shed when the door is opened suddenly; it may well strike in panic. If the person attacks it and tries to kill it, who can blame the cobra for striking in self-defence? Or who can condemn a snake which bites somebody trying to catch it?

In very few cases the snake is the aggressor, and this seems to happen only with the cobras and mambas. Carpet and Burrowing Vipers are better described as bad-tempered: they are not big or fast enough to be aggressive in the above sense.

Whether a snake bite occurs through accident, misunderstanding or aggression, the result is still the same—a quantity of poison has been injected into the body tissues where it will do some damage. The word "strike" is perhaps better than "bite", for it is quite unlike the bite of a cat or dog, for instance. The snake need not close its mouth to bite (except in the case of back-fanged snakes), but can deliver a fatal blow with the mouth open and the fangs exposed. The different types of poison have already been mentioned briefly, but it is well to repeat the important points. Cobras and mambas have comparatively short fangs, always erect, at the front of the upper jaw, and these are very sharp. The venom may be rather small in volume but very potent, and its effect is on the nervous system, particularly on the heart action and breathing. It acts quickly, and death, if it occurs, is generally due to heart failure. Recovery is quick and complete.

In contrast, all vipers have relatively long fangs, fixed to a tiny bone hinged in the front of the upper jaw. These fangs normally lie along the roof of the mouth, but they can instantly swing down and forward into position. Hollow to the tip, they resemble curved hypodermic needles.

Most vipers have a large volume of poison, which may be less concentrated than that of the cobras and mambas, and its chief effect is to destroy the blood cells and certain body tissues, particularly the very small vessels through which the blood flows. This may cause severe internal bleeding, as well as destruction of tissue and death may take place several days after the bite. Full recovery from a severe bite, even if properly and quickly treated, may take weeks. The venom of the Gaboon Viper, and possibly of some other vipers, has also some of the character of cobra venom, making it particularly dangerous.

Several different factors affect the severity of the bite. For various reasons the fangs may not penetrate deeply, or perhaps only one may enter. They may encounter hard skin or other tissue into which the venom can hardly be injected. The snake may have only a reduced supply of venom available or be prevented from injecting a full dose. In addition, the danger and damage normally vary with the size of the victim; that is, for the same amount of venom a child would be in much greater danger than a man twice his weight. One bite may therefore have much more serious results than another.

Effective treatment is drastic and may itself cause shock, so before starting it be quite certain that the victim has been bitten by a *poisonous* snake. The victim's statement may be enough, or he may have killed the snake and brought it in, while the site of the bite, with one or more round punctures, followed by pain, swelling and bleeding, often makes it obvious. If the bite is by any of the back-fanged snakes other than the Boomslang, it is probably best to let well alone and to do neither cutting nor injecting; treat the victim for mild shock and give plenty of fluids. If it can be shown that the victim has been bitten only by a harmless snake with solid teeth, the wounds should be dealt

SNAKE BITE—PREVENTION AND TREATMENT

with merely as cuts or abrasions, but the victim may still need to be treated for shock!

Two things should be done as soon as possible when a serious snake bite has occurred:

1. Remove from the tissues as much as possible of the poison that has been injected. This should be begun on the spot and immediately, for it can mean the difference between life and death.

2. Neutralise the poison already in the system by injecting a serum, called anti-venin, prepared from the blood of horses which have been given artificially a succession of snake bites. For this the victim should be taken to hospital at once.

The first action can be taken by anybody; tie a tight bandage around the limb above the place bitten as near to it as reasonably possible but at a point where the blood can easily be stopped from flowing; take a clean sharp knife or razor blade and make several fairly deep cuts over the place to make it bleed freely. The bandage, properly called tourniquet, stops the poison from being carried into the rest of the body, but it should be loosened every ten or fifteen minutes to allow a little blood to pass and thus prevent the limb from becoming gangrenous. It is not easy to cut oneself deliberately, but it is well worth it, even though it hurts. It is well to remember that a person can lose more than a pint of blood without suffering any harm, and this may remove enough of the venom to save life. Do not cut a main vessel of any kind, either vein or artery.

If the blood does not come freely the wound should be sucked; there is no danger in this unless there is a wound in the mouth or lip, for snake venom is effective only when introduced into the blood stream or in the eye. Many old books recommend rubbing in potassium permanganate, but this does more harm than good. When the area has been cut, wash it with a *weak* solution of potassium permanganate or some other disinfectant.

This first-aid action is known as "cut and suck" treatment and if it is done at once and efficiently the victim will be very unlikely to die. In North America many sportsmen carry small "cut and suck" pocket outfits when hunting or camping in places where there are many dangerous snakes; these consist of razor blades, small glass cups with rubber bulbs for "sucking" the wound and a piece of rubber tubing to make a tourniquet.

The second line of treatment is usually carried out at a hospital, partly because anti-venin must be stored in a refrigerator. Snake poisons vary a great deal, and so it is usual to employ anti-venin which is a mixture of several different kinds; this is called "polyvalent" because it is effective against all or most of the snakes found in any area. One or two small containers of it are injected into the blood stream to neutralise the poison already circulating.

This anti-venin is prepared from horse serum and it is possible for people to suffer from very severe shock or even be killed if they are sensitive to it, though this is more likely in countries where immunisation for diphtheria is practised. In the case of a really severe bite, time is so important that the injection should probably be made at once, but if the bite is only a mild one it might be advisable to do a test for sensitivity before giving a large injection of serum which might cause more damage than the bite itself.

It has now been found that the most effective treatment for victims of giant viper bites, after firstaid and the injection of anti-venin, is the copious administration of blood transfusions or blood serum. This can be done only in hospital.

Postscript: Remember that even without treatment most snake-bite victims recover. Given first-aid treatment the risk of death is very small indeed!